BELFAST
AURORA

BELFAST
AURORA

A MEMOIR OF A FALLS CHILDHOOD,
1971–1973

SEAMUS KELTERS

MERRION
PRESS

First published in 2021 by
Merrion Press
10 George's Street
Newbridge
Co. Kildare
Ireland
www.merrionpress.ie

978 1 78537 414 2 (Cloth)
978 1 78537 415 9 (Ebook)

A CIP catalogue record for this book is available from the
British Library.

Typeset in Sabon LT Pro 11/16

Cover design by Sarah O'Flaherty
Front cover image: courtesy of Brendan Murphy
Back cover image: © Alex Bowie / Collection: Hulton Archive/
Getty images

Merrion Press is a member of Publishing Ireland.

Contents

Acknowledgements

When I wrote these stories I did not know I had cancer. They were prompted by the indefatigable Camilla Carroll, my dearest love, life partner, the mother of our sons, editorial judge beyond comparison.

An American, she suggested that I should set down some of my experiences growing up, to inform our boys. Both journalists, we did not talk politics in front of them simply because we wanted them to reach their own opinions and beliefs without the contamination of our – that is mainly my – interpretation. Camilla persuaded me, with boys now men, that it might be a good time to recount some of our family history and how it sits in broader context.

So I started with what remains one of the most traumatic events, my parents, Jim and Maura Kelters, losing their first real home. It represented emotional and financial investment and their dreams. My father, hit hard that terrible night, somehow emerged without bitterness and never swayed from understanding that we had lost only bricks and mortar where others had lost lives. My mother was shattered mentally and lost forever much of her inward confidence. She needed hospital treatment.

She and my father gave me everything. I was their only child. They spoiled me, a little with material indulgence, but much more with their time, care and unstinting attention. They, and the McAleenan, Collins, Toner and Morris houses that make up my wider family, gifted me so much as I grew, giving advice and a bedrock of absolute security in the most troubled times.

The stories that follow, save for the account of my tonsillectomy and perhaps the barrack bombing, the date of which my research has yet to uncover, sit in chronological order as far as I can recall. I have taken few liberties in the storytelling.

There was no point in altering the names of my immediate family since all are known, nor is there any reason to withhold from history the names of ordinary people who have no one left to remember them. I disguised the names of others because their families may have their own stories stretching beyond the prism of the naive eye of a child or cold analysis of the reporter that I became.

My boys received the work in draft form. Both felt they knew more about their family and if that is all these accounts accomplish then it will be my best achievement. The younger, Michael, who is studying creative writing, gave a visceral and typically kind response. The elder, Brendan, caveated every word with his philosopher's discipline. I am indebted to both for their contributions and for putting up with me as a father.

I am also indebted to a few others who read the text in its crudest form.

The notion to publish came from my dear friend David McKittrick. Kind enough to read the manuscript, he offered many helpful nuances of language and plucked the title from the text. He also kindly agreed to provide a foreword. We and three others, David McVea, Chris Thornton and Brian Feeney, for almost three decades worked on the *Lost Lives* project detailing all deaths directly related to the Troubles.

It was harrowing, but David McKittrick enabled me to cope with many laughs, some tears and never an angry word. He has taught me so much through his kindness, integrity, example and professionalism.

Brendan Murphy, the former picture editor of *The Irish News*, took me under his wing when I began work experience in the paper's newsroom in 1988. He has always sheltered me in my hardest moments in journalism and life. Part surrogate brother and part surrogate father, he has always been ready with sound counsel and that is evidenced throughout *Belfast Aurora* and, indeed, all of my work. He is a giant within Belfast journalism but more so a giant in terms of his decency as a person. He also taught me about how to behave as a reporter and I have always been better for following his advice. He and his wife, Geraldine, have always provided me a much-needed compass and refuge.

Others read the rough draft as well.

I have known Seamus Cleary since we were aged ten. He is a brother to me and although he has half a dozen brilliant siblings, we have shared so much by way of attitude, views and experience. We played football together, served as each other's Best Man and are Godparents to our children. He has been of total support in this text and in life.

Mary McCullough is as close as blood to me, a dear friend, who grew up regarding my father as a big brother and who knows more about my family than me. She offered comment and encouragement and has been a constant sounding board, biased in my favour. Mary has always watched over me through the journey of life. She, and our mutual dearest guide Brigid Malone, added immeasurably to all that I present.

x ♦ BELFAST AURORA

My uncle, Brian Toner, was kind enough to give me the go-ahead to bare family detail. A natural-born teacher who found daily employment in cutting-edge communication technology, he was routinely generous enough to open our history and the city itself to me as I grew up under my grandmother's roof.

My mother-in-law, Donna Carroll, who I love as my own, offered an American eye and her characteristic kindness and unquestioning support.

Mark Gregory, a senior nurse at the cancer centre in Belfast, doubles as a literary troubleshooter for a number of writers and looked at the draft. He too offered immeasurable support during welcome conversations on the text that wonderfully distracted from every chemo session. It is many years since we sat in a school English class together and he has never lost his sharpness, wit or frankness of critique.

Mervyn Jess, a colleague at the BBC and one of the most astute journalists I have ever encountered, is a much-trusted friend. Editorially I have always hated being on the other side of an argument from Mervyn because he is invariably in the right. He was characteristically blunt about the draft. 'Get it finished,' he said, 'and get it out there.' Kathleen Caragher, my boss and Head of News at BBC Northern Ireland, has also been most encouraging. Both have my profound thanks.

Another family, the Cronins, permeate these pages. John Cronin, who sadly passed away just as I finished writing, was the former head of English at Queen's University. I never knew him in an academic capacity but rather as the father of a quartet of close friends. He constantly encouraged me to believe I might have something worthwhile to say through the written word. His wife, Joan, taught me English at school, helping me hone an awareness of the power of language. Much more than a teacher, she became a very unerring friend. One of her three sons, Nick, was a classmate at Rathmore Grammar School. Now living in Ohio, running libraries and still kicking a football, he has always been a most generous supporter of my work. His brother, Michael, lectures in English literature in Italy and, despite a disciplined and incredibly busy life, he unselfishly offered to proofread and take on the unenviable task of touting the work to potential publishers.

The Cronin family, all of them, have been constant treasures to me and without them these words would never have made the pages.

One other teacher from Rathmore examined the draft. When I first, and somewhat accidentally, started at that school situated in woodland atop a small hill, it was as though I had moved to the countryside rather than the outskirts of Belfast. Adjacent to a convent in a grand house, once the home of shipyard owners, it was alien to all of my experience in the terraced streets of the Falls. For the first six months I would be laughed at because every time I saw a bird in the air I ducked my head. The only thing that seemed to be in the air at St Paul's were stones. With the formidable principal, the late Sister Joan Lynam, and fellow teachers, Eamonn Hamill, Gerry Devanney, Mrs Kearney, Sister Margaret and the sorely missed Martin Donaghy and Miss McCann, Henry McNally helped me settle to myself. More than anyone else, a teacher of sociology by trade, he encouraged me to find my voice.

I was always welcomed in his home by him and his dear wife, Ita. He was kind enough to read the manuscript and was as always most supportive. Thanks to Henry, I started to order and measure my words. My parents loved him for his honesty and integrity, and, in forty years of friendship, he has never been less than an inspiration.

I am indebted also to Liam Andrews who unearthed and supplied me with the Hansard extract regarding my grandfather.

The others who deserve my acknowledgement are the people I have attempted to detail in these pages. Many are no longer here, but all existed and endured, with humour and grace, the travails of poverty and violence that tumbled over them as waves on a choppy sea. They are the people of my part of Belfast and I am sure their character can be found in those classed as ordinary in any part of my city, the country or the world. They are the people who add flavour to life.

Any flaws in this book are my responsibility and have nothing to do with any of those who saw the drafts. I will admit to altering only the endings of the stories centred on my primary school. This was partly to compress events and partly to attempt to add to a more natural narrative edge where, if you like, memories are slightly embellished. These are the only places where I depart in any way from fact. Where these few accounts see endings amended, all other stories are stated exactly as happened as intimately and imperfectly as recollection allows.

My thanks end where they began, with my darling wife. She has held me through every word and phrase, every trial and disputation and the good times and the bad. How she has done that while working in her own right as a modest but multi-award-winning reporter and producer, as well as rearing our boys while I absented myself to a variety of work projects, I will never know.

I do know that with the cancer, inoperable as I have been told it is, my future appears more uncertain. Ironically perhaps, I count myself fortunate for the blessing through this of extended family, friends, colleagues and strangers too many to mention, even though all should know the tremendous value in their many conversations, visits and kindnesses, as well as their stream of supportive texts, emails and cards.

Most of all my boys and my Camilla sustain and provide meaning. Without her I would not have written. Without her I would not be surviving. Without her I would not have the strength to either publish or attempt to prevail. She has always been the source of any of my strength.

The words thanks and love are too small for her, Brendan and Michael and all of the others mentioned named and nameless as well, of course, as my mother and father and the wholly unique generation that went before us.

Seamus Kelters, September 2017

Foreword

It's hard to know how to start describing my old pal Seamus Kelters, because he was not only a great friend but also a great journalist and storyteller. And – to top it all – he can, without exaggeration, be described as a great human being.

As is evident in his writings, Seamus was something special. Although he was himself a child of the Northern Ireland Troubles, he immersed himself as a leading member of the team of five which produced *Lost Lives*, the book which chronicled the thousands of deaths in the conflict.

When the rest of us in that team sometimes felt like giving up that sombre task, Seamus was unflagging, providing the impetus to keep going. He was the heart of the group.

But in addition to chronicling the violence which has now thankfully diminished, he was also a writer of exceptional charm and insight. His writings in this work capture the goodness of many in Northern Ireland in a way which few other works have managed. It displays his humour, his insights and, underlying it all, a natural deep humanity which survived all those terrible troubles.

Belfast had many heroes and many villains, but it only ever had one Seamus Kelters.

David McKittrick, July 2021

Camera

Lured by the vibrancy of the times and verdancy of the place, my parents bought a house, newly built, on what was once a sloping grazed field on the side of Divis Mountain. My mother kept the paperwork for years – the site plan, the deposit receipt, the letter dated February 1966 confirming purchase. My grandmother tried to persuade them not to buy. She did not like the area. There were no shops and only the one bus. It was almost outside the city. (In fact, it was not much more than a mile away even by the most circuitous route.) Most of all, this was Belfast, what would happen if the Troubles started again?

'Don't be silly,' my mother told her, 'it's the 1960s.'

My new playground was the building site where the remaining houses were under construction. One child broke fingers when a block fell during a weekend exploration. Warned not to go there, for us this naturally added to the attraction.

If we were drawn to the bricks and the fantasy world we could create with them, the adults were drawn to the gardens. These were the physical proof that they had somehow risen beyond the claustrophobic terraces. Of a summer's evening, they would sow seeds, ferry wheelbarrows and all manner of tools borrowed from neighbours, and exchange plant slips over new fences. In such a way they grew community.

Near the first crook of the uppermost bend, our house was on one of the steeper inclines. The battle for my parents, it seemed to me, was to level the front garden. Potatoes were planted in that first year to break down the clay. My father took a picture of her, my mother, kneeling, weeding, when the plants were at their height. It was beautifully innocent, taken with the only thing of value he ever bought for himself. For years, he had put coppers aside before buying the Voigtlander Bessa, a post-war German model made with considerable ingenuity. When he was out, I would sometimes gingerly fold it out of its case, extend its leathery bellows, feel the quality of the metal clicks around its lens and look through its viewfinder at a framed world.

Exposed films were treated with reverence and then there was that wonderfully excruciating wait before the pictures could be picked up from the chemist's. We would pore over them for hours and my father would hold the negatives up to the light, examining each detail of the printing and edges. His favourite pictures were of my mother: motionless in front of a waterfall in the Glens of Antrim; standing during their honeymoon in Galway like a film star in her mackintosh among the cattle dealers at Maam Cross market. When he took the picture of my mother weeding, he was standing at the door of their new home. Below in the front garden, she, young and happy in one of his old white shirts, was all that broke the pattern of the drill rows.

Surplus potatoes were given to neighbours, who in turn shared turnips, peas and carrots. An old farmer lived in a row of little cottages on the front of the main road. The shiny number nine bus stop was a few yards from his front door. He struck up a conversation with my mother as she waited and it emerged he had gathered hay, grown flax and tended livestock on the very land where our house now stood. Within weeks, she was bringing him occasional bags of groceries and he gave her tomato plants, which seemed somehow more exotic. I remember my mother one day saying to him, 'The times are changing.' He shrugged his shoulders.

'It's not the times,' he told her, 'it's the people.'

The masterstroke of the builder and estate agent was simply in finding a name. Years later, pretending a posh accent, a neighbour who lived there would declare, 'We lived in Springfield Park.' All the emphasis was on the final word. Their identity was no longer in the name of a street. The very word 'park' seemed to reinforce the gardens and greenery, which separated them from their red-brick roots. Everyone who lived there called it 'the park'.

New families arriving by the week and the construction finally finishing forced us children across a stream running along the back of houses opposite. The field there now became our playground. An old air-raid shelter, overgrown into the stream bank, gave us a cavern where the ultimate dare was to brave the cobwebs to touch the furthest wall.

Only in summer would we venture higher to the top of Divis. Picking steps to find paths through the undergrowth, we scarcely looked behind; three or four of the men and maybe a dozen children brought out from underfoot of their mothers. Rabbits scuttled before us, their tails blinking white above the heather. They would easily outrun any of our dogs. At the top, we would eat ham sandwiches and drink watery orange cordial produced out of some bags carried by the fathers. These rituals completed, it was as though the view was suddenly unveiled.

Below in the city, the most dominant structures were the shipyard cranes. The big yellows of Samson and Goliath stood out against the steely blues, greens and greys of Belfast Lough. Scotland's mountains laced the horizon in dim outline. My father had relatives there and would tell of his visits to Glasgow. He pointed to Donard, the highest of the Mournes to the south and, just beyond, the mountains of the Cooley Peninsula, where he had spent childhood holidays. Usually the trek would be on a Sunday when there was little port traffic, a couple of smoke trails from boats hardly streaking.

The Castlereagh Hills rose less dramatically on the far side of the Lagan basin, Stormont's Portland stone like a little off-white toy brick, the parliament's building. No one referred to it, a place synonymous with unionist rule. Behind it, further south, was the turret of Scrabo tower, a Victorian memorial to some Napoleonic-era general.

Beneath us, much closer, was the merged greenery of the two cemeteries, the City and Milltown, the Falls Park and the marshes of the Bog Meadows. Spires needling up from the flat land of the city gave it the appearance of a pincushion. The men would pick out the church landmarks where they had been baptised and married. Dwarfed by a new high-rise block, the pro-cathedral's almost twin spires were easy to identify. Sometimes we would have been there or to the monastery that morning, calling in with relatives or friends along the way home. However, with the opening of a new church, Corpus Christi, close by on the other side of the main Springfield Road, we tended to opt more for convenience. One of its curates, a balding, inoffensive man, lived in our street. Some neighbours went separate ways to an arc of churches from the Shankill and Woodvale districts right across to the Springfield Road and beyond, but I never thought long about this as a child, for churches were somewhere you went on Sunday mornings. Casement, Corrigan, McCrory Park, the Gaelic sports grounds, gardens, the field and sometimes, on the best of days, the mountain were for Sunday afternoons.

Sounds, incredibly clear, rolled up the slopes. We could hear the rattle of the Dublin train, a distant millipede heading out of the city. There was always a small triumph in being first to sight it and then we would all share intermittent glimpses between breaks in the terraces. One year in June we went up on a Friday evening and the flute notes of Orange bands sounded close. 'That's down the Shankill so it is,' said one of the adults. My father agreed. 'The mad month's coming,' was all he said, and I did not understand.

So steep in appearance from the city, Divis rolls gently away on the other side towards Lough Neagh, five counties making up its shoreline. To the west, the Sperrins form an impressive curtain. In later years, I would learn the names of the tops: Mullaghcarn, Sawel and Slieve Gallion. To the north, Slemish, where Patrick tended sheep, looked like a misplaced button. Yet for all the grand variety of this vista, invariably scrutinised through a pair of binoculars owned by one of the fathers, the eyes would gradually be drawn to the little horseshoe of houses directly below us, where all would single out their own chimney pots, rooftops and gardens. Sometimes one of the wives would be spied through the looking glasses and all the men would start laughing at being able to see them tend the clothes lines.

Dancing on the line in our back garden were my father's coal-grey dungarees. One of the others joked about another man being out the back of our house. These men were becoming easy in each other's company now. We took turns with the binoculars. I got to see. Every week my mother washed those dungarees. By the end of the week, they would again smell of sweat, oil and metal. My father's first day in long trousers had been the day after he turned fourteen, the day he started in the big engineering factory where, three decades later, he continued to work.

He never took the camera to the mountain. It was not heavy. I supposed he did not want to risk damage. It was reserved for birthdays, holidays and when friends were round. On some occasions, he would bring out flash bulbs, holding them almost as carefully as the camera itself. Tiny glassy affairs, they fitted in front of a fan of little mirrors that in turn attached somehow to the top of the Voigtlander. They would briefly blind their subjects in a burst of magnesium blue. Afterwards I would play with them, imagining all sorts of jewelled space rays. Holding them up to the window, the break in the filament was clear and sometimes the inside of the vacuum was stained black.

Perhaps he did not take the camera to the mountain because he felt Belfast not worth picturing. In all the strips of negatives, none were of the city where he lived his life. It might accidentally creep into the background, yet every image was of friends and family. The city had no wonder for him; it was never an object of reflection.

As rain spat on our rooftops, the women scrambled like army ants to pull washing from back-garden lines. Buttressed tight against the rise of the mountain, the street itself only had views in one direction. Those on the Castlereagh side of the city could see squalls approaching for miles before they struck. When storms came, because we were fast under the black back of Divis, we would be last to learn of their approach.

Summer storms became mainly man-made, rumbling and crackling their way up from the terraces and rolling in from the sprawling new estates. Troubles had come again to Belfast, this city of history, hard men and hatred.

Everywhere of an evening you would feel the argument of politics. People began to mention religion, Protestant and Catholic. I asked my father about this. He told me we were Catholics and that people, no matter what religion they were, were all the same. I was confused. Once he brought me to a demonstration and, perched on his shoulders, I heard a thousand solemn voices sing 'We Shall Overcome'. In a street near where I was born, from the back of a low lorry, a man gave an angry speech, waved a flag of green, white and orange, and shouted 'United Ireland or nothing'. The crowd roared. That man, years later, would wear ermine in the House of Lords. My father quietly watched. I sensed even then he was unconvinced by politicians. 'Treat people as you find them,' he said, 'treat them the way they treat you and never judge anyone by his creed, colour or class.'

I did not understand then what he meant. The only creed I knew was the one we said weekly in Mass. Everybody in Belfast, apart from one family in Springfield Park, was the same colour. Our worst enemies in school were in the other classes and we judged ourselves against them daily every which way. Still, I nodded, for my father had that seriousness to him when he told me this and I realised he intended it as something to be held close.

He was a dues-paid Transport and General man in a firm that would not employ trade unionists. He spoke for the Faller Shop. A battery of deafening drilling machines, it was in a place where, in the whole time he worked there, no Catholic was ever given a brown coat, a foreman's position. James Mackie & Sons was about a mile down the Springfield Road. My father bought his *Irish News* and consumed it every day at lunch, where the majority of those alongside him digested the unionist paper, the *News Letter*. 'Never be afraid to stand up for what you believe in,' was another thing he said. He was on the residents' committee, coached football, table tennis and boxing in a youth club, helped found a Credit Union – a community banking co-operative – and, aged forty-four, began taking part in vigilante patrols aiming to maintain 'the park' as a calm haven from the approaching tempest.

Unusual in so far as it was a new city development inhabited by both Protestants and Catholics, both religions took their places side by side in the patrols. In reality, they could do little but observe events push towards their boundaries. The father of the Indian family, a hospital consultant in the Royal Victoria, took part in the patrols as well. On an evening when CS gas drifted on the air along with distant yells, someone asked him how he explained what was going on to people back home. 'I tell them the natives are restless,' he said with a shave of a smile.

Walks to the mountain became less frequent. The last time we were there, the men spoke more seriously. They were pointing to a new estate springing from green fields behind our street. Geography was not in their favour. The new estate, built to take the overflow from the staunchly unionist Shankill, had some high rises on the crest of the slope overlooking the back of 'the park'. On the other side of the main road was Ballymurphy. By 1970, packed with families streaming up from the staunchly nationalist Falls, it was already acquiring a reputation making it synonymous with strife. Springfield Park, as one neighbour put it, was 'the jam in the sandwich'.

On the surface and in daylight 'the park' remained with its version of normality. On weekdays most headed off to their workplaces. My parents still worked to level the garden. At weekends, neighbours chatted and went to parties in each other's houses. The Saturday night in 1970 when Dana won the Eurovision Song Contest, they went out to their gates, celebrating with an impromptu version of 'All Kinds of Everything'.

All machines, my father would say, have their tolerance points, the upper limit which, when exceeded, everything would break. Belfast exceeded its tolerance point in those years, though few realised it at the time. Everywhere it seemed as if the abnormal had become commonplace: riots and shooting, angry voices and shouts, buses burning and barricades. This was all accepted with hardly a second thought.

Adults at first tried to shield us from the sound of gunfire, smoky breezes and the images they clustered around nightly on the television news. Then they gave up, as it all became part of the daily rhythm. We saw soldiers with helmets, guns and armoured cars, and acted out in our play what we saw on the charred skeletons of bread-van barricades on our way to and from school.

Bigger things were happening. There was shooting across the monastery garden and nearby Catholic homes were burned. Those responsible included some of my father's workmates. The IRA torched big mills on the Falls, turning the night sky red with sparks. Orangemen on the march passed Ballymurphy. Bands played sectarian songs. Soldiers hemmed in incensed residents. They rioted. Closer to home, we felt the heat.

On a direct line between Ballymurphy and the new loyalist estate, Springmartin, the row of cottages by the bus stop was burned. My father and some of the others were listening to police transmissions on a radio. 'Houses on fire at Springfield Park,' the voice crackled. 'Houses on fire at Springfield Park. Over.' They ran from their card game, looking for flames to the far end of the street nearest Springmartin, only to see them instead coming from the little line fronting the main road. The fires were probably set by the IRA to give themselves a clear line of defence and attack. 'There was nothing we could do,' said my father. 'The fire brigade and police were there but there was nothing they could do either.'

Until it rained, for days warmth came from the rubble smoulders. The bus sign was melted like candy. I asked where the old farmer had gone, if he was safe. My mother shrugged. I could see she was frustrated at not being able to answer, having to tell me she did not know.

That last summer, they painted the window frames and

the front door, my father bringing them up to a high gloss sheen. A friend, who was a decorator, balanced on one leg of a ladder to reach the eaves. My parents thought of putting the house up for sale but decided, as they put it, to 'stick it out and see whether things settled down'. Looking back, I think they would have seen leaving as a betrayal of neighbours. They still worked on the garden, lowering it almost level. That seemed to be their release and relaxation, and they took real pride in the changes. The potatoes were gone. In the centre of a well-tended lawn they had planted an ornamental cherry tree. My father would use a push-mower with a heavy roller given to them by a man who left for Australia.

'I can't take it anymore,' he told my mother and father. 'It's not going to get better so it's not.'

He was right. They were wrong.

The end came quickly: one night, 9 August 1971. After weeks of confrontation, the Stormont government was desperate and, in its desperation, sought London's approval and military muscle for the one measure that it hoped would restore order. Internment, imprisonment without trial, was introduced, 300 Catholics arrested in a series of early morning swoops. Ballymurphy, as ever, was in the forefront. My father set out for work but turned back when he heard about the raids. 'Internment's in' was all he said. He and my mother discussed what to do and then they joined the others at their gateposts talking through the implications of events.

By lunchtime, the debate was becoming academic. Large crowds from Ballymurphy and Springmartin taunted each other across the main road. Soldiers who had reinforced a church hall near the bottom of our street with barbed wire and sandbags were edging trigger fingers, trying to communicate with outlying patrols scattered around the district. What few police there were on the ground were never going to hold back the crowds and by that stage most Catholics saw them simply as the armed extension of Protestant mobs. An appeal for calm from the curate was greeted by jeers.

The first flights of stones, like some portage of medieval arrows, came over the rise from Springmartin, hitting the back of houses in Springfield Park. Windows smashed. Everywhere was panic. Some ran with children, some ran with bottles and stones, and some just ran. The main road was far too dangerous, so the field where we played became the only escape route for terrified adults trying to shepherd their children to safety. Families streamed across the little river's stepping-stones, taking with them all the belongings they could carry.

A small group of men, my father included, had to use a chair to lift an eighty-year-old woman over back hedges. All the while, they watched soldiers taking up position, aiming their rifles from the rooftops of the Springmartin high rises. Not long after, a loyalist crowd, emboldened by the lack of resistance and frustrated by the even match on the main road, started to come through the back fences of houses at the top end of the street, yelling and whooping to announce their presence.

There are many versions of who fired the first shot. As good as any is the account that has an IRA man venturing into Springfield Park and shooting his pistol over the heads of the mob from Springmartin. My father always said he did not know. Someone in a group attacking the upper end of Springfield Park produced a shotgun and fired at fleeing residents. My father was running towards the cover of our home with the baby of a neighbour who was a couple of paces behind with another child by the hand and another in his arms. The neighbour took the worst of the blast, but my father was hit as well. Soldiers in the church hall fired repeatedly, scything down civilians on the Ballymurphy side of the road. They killed two men, fatally wounded another and shot dead a mother of eight.

In the field, a woman stood still, paralysed with fear. Another neighbour was crawling in the tall grass. The soldiers on top of the high rises fired at him, searing a gouge across the small of his back. He screamed from the pain. The priest's house was opposite. He saw the wounded man and went to him waving a white cloth. The soldiers shot him. In the field where we played, the soldiers shot him. He got up on one knee. They shot him again. A man trying to help was killed as well. Others carried away the bodies on doors used as makeshift stretchers. High velocity rounds ploughed furrows through the earth of the field where we played.

In our home, my mother and father and some forty neighbours lay on the floor. It was one of only two houses safe in terms of the angles of fire. The unpredictable acoustic ebbed and flowed in waves hitting the distant streets; the pings and whines rattled our very slates. Like the face of an amplifier, the mountain vibrated back each crack, smack and roar. One round spat through the metal coal bunker at our back door.

At dawn, save for a baby crying and the bark of a distant dog, there was silence.

'There had been that much shooting I thought there would be bodies all over the street,' my mother said.

The morning lull was followed by more chaos. People fled. Flatbed trucks were arriving, taking away box loads and bedding to 'refugee centres', the term suggesting some element of organisation where none existed. My father carried what he could up and down to the lorry sitting at the gate. It collected our clothing and some light furniture, bric-a-brac covering boxes where a few items of real value were buried. While my father put his arm around my mother, the truck pulled away, a mix of two families sitting on top of detritus shouting instructions and directions to relatives running along behind.

The following nights were spent on the floor of my grandmother's house. All of us lay on mattresses brought down from bedrooms judged too vulnerable to the gunfire. It started just before dusk. We saw some tracers, high and harmless. Oddly peaceful amidst the shooting, the army fired a couple of flares. Hung from parachutes, the flares dragged phosphorous false daylight across the sky. In their brief flickering light, I saw the pickled bruise marks of the shotgun pellets on my father's back, his skin just broken.

It took three days for things to calm sufficiently for them to get the information to go and retrieve our belongings. The 'refugee centre' was a primary school in one of the estates beyond the Falls. It rained steadily, a dank steamy summer rain. Families were scattered across the school hall on bedding of all shapes and sizes. There were a few boxes there, but nothing of my parents. As they left, my mother remarked on some rags piled in the corner of the schoolyard. 'God help whoever owns those,' she said.

Then she noticed, on top of a sodden coat, a tiny item familiar to her, a softstone sculpture of the Virgin Mary. It had belonged to my father's mother. Its glass dome sat alongside, undamaged. My mother pulled away the rags. They were my father's dungarees. Underneath were a few things we had owned. Most, though, was gone, looted. My parents returned to my grandmother's house carrying two boxes. A few toys, a few photographs and some cutlery, including an apostle spoon given by my grandmother, were all there was to salvage from more than a dozen years of married life.

'We got out alive son and that's all that matters,' my father said.

It was two months before my mother told me that my father's camera was one of the items stolen. He never took another picture.

Meat

My grandparent's house was close to my school, so I stayed there Sunday to Thursday nights, six years of that routine coinciding with the height of the Troubles. Early on, my parents decided it was better for me to be there, in the heart of the Falls, rather than in our home, which was becoming increasingly vulnerable. Once, when the shooting kept going for days, my grandmother moved out, bringing me to an aunt's home in the Ormeau district so we could 'get a break'. Four nearby houses were petrol bombed in as many days. We moved back to Cavendish Street. Danger there was mainly due to its particular location, looking almost straight up a leg of 'the square' towards the back of the barracks. Heavy fortification seemed to attract the IRA, who were forever taking pot-shots from every conceivable angle when least expected. Riots and attacks on soldiers' foot patrols were an almost daily occurrence, but there was no factional strife so, in the bizarre world of early seventies' Belfast, it felt somehow safer.

From that house I had already witnessed history. In August 1969, I saw petrol bombs thrown at the barracks. Hands under my chin at the end of the bed, with a cousin and my grandfather beside me, we watched B-Specials gather in the street. In their long black coats and shiny peaked helmets, like so many crows they swooped up the square in a pincer move designed to trap a handful of the teenagers throwing Molotov cocktails. Anyone caught would be whisked off to jail. The statutory penalty was marked in one of the protest chants of the time: 'What do we want? Civil rights. What do we get? Six months.'

The front room downstairs, always called the parlour, had a bay window. A few days after the riot, I was sitting at the piano when there was an unusual whine in the street. Small, unmistakably military, a four-wheeled, olive-green armoured car trundled past, left to right, heading for the main road. Running to the adults in the other room, almost speechless, I tried to describe what I had just witnessed. They were gathered around the television clinging to a bulletin. They told me to be quiet, 'The news is on, the army's in.' They did not realise the army was outside.

This was August 1969.

It was all cups of tea, cake and biscuits for the soldiers then; hard to believe a few months later. On a Sunday they held band parade in Cavendish Square, right in the middle of the street between the barracks and my old school; the full dress uniforms, dark blue, red stripes, white pith helmets, all silvery and brassy as they played their strange hymns. A few years older than us, soldiers played football in the square with the local youngsters, some of them my classmates.

I was the only one forbidden, my grandfather's decision. He was from near Crossmaglen, a village that defied every attempt to impose outside authority. 'They're playing with them now, they'll be shooting them soon enough,' said my grandfather. He was right, and he was also right in saying that when guns come out, they would not be put away again for a long time.

If the backdrop was mayhem, the reality was that being a child in those times of craziness was a happy existence.

My grandmother's home drew a miscellany of family, friends and neighbours. The talk, those summer nights, always concentrated on politics. Programmes watched with most reverence were always the debates. Often there could be up to nine or ten people crammed into the tiny back room hanging on the words. There would be pin-drop silence when someone they agreed with was speaking, shouts and shushes when it was a unionist or British politician.

Debate on television would always be followed by debate in the room. They rehearsed the arguments that should have been aired, contesting those they found disagreeable, disprovable, distasteful. I began to think debating an adult occupation. Conclusions, like the television, were always black and white. Sandwiches, buns and my grandmother's apple cake would circulate with cups of tea, each person attempting to balance saucers and little plates, the good delft, on their knees. Voices would settle. The pair of cats would stretch in front of the fire. There would be stories, laughter, maybe another news bulletin, this time from the radio, before someone would say, 'Oh look at the time', and they would leave for their own homes.

It would always be some variation of the same crowd, mostly featuring my uncles and father and mother, with neighbours well represented. Periodic guests would be the two sisters who lived in the square, the woman who ran the little home bakery around the corner, and Paddy Joe, who was a family friend.

More regular would be Mrs Smith from a few doors down. She was close to my grandmother. From Portadown direction, she had come to Belfast as a young girl to work in one of the mills. She met John, a bread server in Hughes' bakery. He came from a few townlands away across the border in Cavan. They married and remained in the city to raise their family in a little two-up two-down. I never knew Mrs Smith's first name. My grandmother, who must have known her for thirty years, referred to her only ever as 'Mrs Smith'. A quietly spoken, timid woman, she gave every impression of being intimidated by the harshness of Belfast, its accent, its divisions. Rarely would she utter a word during any discussion. If she did, it would be only to say, 'That's terrible.' It usually was, of course, yet it was as if not being from the city she felt no right to enter the darkness of its reality. Unless there was some huge upheaval, John would not be there after nine o'clock as he would be getting up early to do his morning route. Politics were never his priority. In his little battery-powered van, he trundled through the streets before dawn ensuring loaves were left beside milk bottles on the doorsteps. Like his wife, he took no truck with the Troubles and would not allow even barricades or smouldering fires to knock him off schedule.

As loud as Mrs Smith was quiet, Philly Savage was a big, barnstorming woman. She had been at school with my grandmother and, with my grandfather, was the only other person who would call her Jeannie. As both friends went for the same jobs there were raised eyebrows, for my grandmother's maiden name was Christian. The names were somehow appropriate. Philly Savage voiced her opinions enthusiastically, holding her own in any debate. Her first and last name always rolled into one, her married name was not mentioned. Whispered among the adults, never in her presence, was that her husband had been a gunman in the twenties. He would accompany her frequently. As jolly as his wife, Sean would roar with laughter at jokes. On the occasions when he would offer opinion, his voice was soft and the others would listen. Examining him carefully I could see no sign that this cheery, grandfatherly man had ever carried anything more imposing than his big slouch hat. It would be placed upon arrival on the hallway coat hooks. Once, dared by a cousin when the door to the hall was closed, I tried it on. As it enveloped my head, the cousin laughed so loudly I felt sure we would be discovered.

Mrs Martin, another of those without a first name, came from Earlscourt Street, one of the streets branching off Cavendish Street. Other streets had the names of flowers and plants: Violet, Crocus, Iris and Hawthorn. Travelling those streets, I was sure whoever named them had never lived in their hard rows.

I never knew anything of Mrs Martin's origins, or how she came to know my grandmother. Standing at over six feet tall, lean, long-limbed and angular, she strode, an eye-catching figure wearing an ankle-length coat and, habitually, a 1920s-style flapper's bonnet. More improbably, until a relatively recent accident, she had been the proud owner of a motorcycle and sidecar. Her sister, a tiny woman called Teasie, had accompanied her in the sidecar, although never to my grandmother's house. Their biking adventures had apparently come to an abrupt halt when the last bolt holding together sidecar and machine sheered while cornering, sending Teasie travelling clean through a hedge. My grandmother had tried to recount what had happened sympathetically, but even she was reduced to choking laughter at the thought of a dumbstruck Teasie coming to rest in a sheugh. I met Teasie only a few times when my grandmother bumped into her and Mrs Martin at the shops on the front of the road. I never heard her speak.

Mrs Martin's contributions to the political discourse were pointed. 'These men haven't a clue,' she would say. Other times it would be, 'There are no real men to finish this business.' The men in the room would shift uncomfortably. I never ever heard any reference to Mr Martin. I wondered had he been dispatched to 'finish the business'. I tried to ask what 'the business' was; she flashed me a tolerant smile and continued to press her case. I was unsure why, but I feared her. I suspected my grandfather felt the same way.

Of all the visitors, though, it was Tommy O'Rawe who I studied most carefully. At around forty-five, a confirmed bachelor, I could never figure if he was closer in age to seventy-five or fifteen. He had been at the old school in the square with my uncles. He lived diagonally across the street. He had known my grandmother all his life and never referred to her as anything other than Mrs Toner. First his mother, then his father had died when he was still young. My grandmother had helped take care of the family. One by one his siblings married and left home. Now Tommy was in the house alone. More often, though, he would be in my grandmother's. Even as a child I saw that he would time his arrival, two or three nights a week, to coincide with meals. My grandmother provided dinner or, on a Sunday night, a salad tea for Tommy, welcoming him as her own. He paid tribute to the food. 'You're a great cook altogether Mrs Toner,' he would say and, smiling, she would respond with an 'Ah Tommy.'

If Tommy had work, it was a mystery to me. He did not speak of a job. Sometimes, when my uncles would talk about their work, I would see him ever so slightly blanch. He would speak with most eagerness to my grandfather of his visits to the billiards tables at Clonard in the AOH hall. When my grandmother came into the room the topic would change smoothly, both men anticipating her disapproval. It was unclear to me whether it was the billiards or the AOH that most displeased her. I asked once what the letters stood for. 'Ancient Order of Hibernians,' she told me, 'the Catholic Orange Order.'

Tommy spoke in a peculiar high-pitched gurgle suggestive of some oesophageal ailment. During political debates, I noticed, he was the best thermometer in terms of the temperature of the room, jeering unionists louder than anyone else and affecting a fervent hush when a nationalist, any nationalist, was speaking. When a point was well made, he rocked back in his chair and clapped his hands together, appreciation spilling over into raw excitement. His laugh yelped around the tiny room, occasionally startling the cats into darting under the seats or out of the room. So animated would Tommy become, so eager to conform, that I would find myself concentrating on him more than anything on the television.

'You are right there Mr Toner,' he would say when my grandfather would make some comment.

My grandfather was a big-boned butcher. Born on the Shankill Road but raised near Hackballscross, between the counties of Armagh and Louth, he came back to Belfast at the age of thirteen or fourteen, a raw country lad, to work in the family's butcher shops. Most weekday evenings he would produce from his coat a dripping, bloody brown-paper parcel of meat; mince, liver, stewing steak or perhaps sausages if he had made them himself. Of a Friday evening there would always be a big black pudding for a fry on Saturday and a prime silverside cut for a Sunday roast.

I was not at those weekend meals when Tommy was often at the table. My grandfather, who gave the appearance of enjoying his company, was simple in his politics and it struck me that he liked having Tommy's unswerving vindication. Indeed, if any of the visitors demurred from the consensus of the household, Tommy would side with his hosts. It was impossible not to think of him as some sort of court jester. Even in my earliest memory, I, the young prince, only ever called him Tommy and, for his part, answered loyally, going along with my whims and naiveté. The first adult to ever agree with anything I said about politics, he did not question noble positions on the matter of the day's events. 'It was murder, plain and simple Mr Toner. You are right there,' he would tell my grandfather again. The cats seemed to sense that they were above Tommy in the pecking order and, after a short time, they would resume their places flexing by the fire.

Of all the occupants of my grandmother's house, it was only the cats that made Tommy uncomfortable. Should they come near, he sniffed nervously. If they sleeked against him, he shivered. He did not seem to be allergic so much as fearful. 'Ma', the big tortoiseshell, would circle Tommy, who shrank into his chair. Tommy eyed her warily as she arched her back, flicked her tail and swanked by his seat. This provided me with great entertainment. A couple of times I brought 'Ma' into the room stealthily to release her close to Tommy in the hope she would hone in on her target. Sometimes she ignored him, but on those occasions when she approached him, he always recoiled. 'Ma' did not like Tommy and Tommy did not like 'Ma'. For my grandmother's sake, it appeared, both agreed to an uneasy truce.

There was no truce outside on the street, not between the IRA and the British army and police. The bomb at the barracks should not have been a surprise. The walls were reinforced concrete. The blast impact tangled and pierced some corrugated metal shielding but left the building otherwise undamaged. Shock waves bounced into surrounding streets, like when the coal man emptied a bag into the coal hole. My grandmother's house was directly in line. Glass, some metal and dust showered the whole front of the house. Big and small, every window came in and the cats jumped over the high wall at the back, staying away for hours. Remarkably, no one was badly hurt. It was just after lunch on a Sunday.

In less than an hour an army of amateur glaziers and handymen were putting putty and panes back or hammering in boards where the frames needed more work. The sash windows in the front bay took five days to repair. About twenty houses in total were damaged, the half-dozen closest to the bomb wrecked. Arriving as the dust was still rising, I was employed in a variety of the meaningless tasks given to children to keep them from harm's way. All the while, as the men worked at the front, my grandmother was brushing away shovelfuls of shards and splinters, dumping them noisily in the back-entry bins.

That evening the cats returned and Tommy appeared. He had been away at his sister's for dinner, showing up around the usual time for tea. 'Ah Mrs Toner, it's terrible. It's terrible. Are you alright?'

It emerged that one small window at the back of Tommy's house had cracked, a vagary of the ways of the blast wave. 'I might leave it, sure it's not too bad. Just a wee drop of tea in my hand's fine so it is. Sure I'm still shaking. I'm sure you got a shock.'

My grandmother looked exhausted. She had been in the scullery when the bomb went off and my grandfather had been sitting in his usual seat when the glass from the doors avalanched up the hall. There was no hint from her of anything unusual. Twenty minutes earlier, as she portioned a tin of Kit-e-Kat food for 'Ma' and the other cat, I had watched a single tear carve through the dust on her cheek. Then I saw her eyes narrow the way they did when she threaded a needle. She wetted her finger as she bent to pick up a sliver of glass that had somehow fallen from her shovel. The empty tin sat where it had been forgotten on the sideboard.

'I'll have tea for you in a minute Tommy,' she said.

'Ma' eyed Tommy. Tommy eyed 'Ma'. Both were nervous following the explosion. The only difference was that he was also nervous about her, whereas she was not at all nervous about him.

My grandfather buckled into his chair. 'Terrible Mr Toner. Terrible all together.' Tommy was chattering. I could tell my grandfather was weary by the way he sighed.

He would sigh like that and sink into the seat after a particularly busy day in the shop.

The news came on the television and all activity ceased.

'A bomb's exploded outside Springfield Road police station. Soldiers and police escaped injury but one woman living nearby was taken to hospital. Her condition's not known.'

Someone said this was Mrs Hayes 'up in the square' and all nodded in agreement.

An uncle said he had seen her get into the back of a car.

'She wasn't too bad, bit of a cut on her arm.'

'Glass,' said someone else.

All spoke simultaneously.

A few pictures came on screen. For the briefest moment the camera pointed down the square and caught one of my uncles and another neighbour measuring up the board on the front bay. A big cheer went up in the room.

'There's our house,' shouted my grandfather.

'It is Mr Toner. It is,' cackled Tommy. 'Ma' bolted under the settee.

After the news, a religious programme came on with hymns. Talk went to the bomb. The bomb was a bad idea. The bomb could have killed someone. The bomb was in 'the wrong place'. No one said anything about the IRA. I cannot recall my grandfather speaking. I do remember Tommy agreeing with him. 'You are right there Mr Toner. You are surely.'

My grandmother began to ferry tea from the kitchen. Food had been destroyed by the dusty film that had descended on everything. She had thrown out the cut of silverside, still cooling on a dish, that was to have been used for the 'pieces' put in Monday's lunch boxes. With Tommy arriving and one of the glaziers accepting the invitation to take 'a wee bite', she had to dive deep into the scullery cupboard. There she had found it; a tin of corned beef. In a house where only fresh meat was served, it was a novelty on the plate. If Tommy had encountered corned beef previously there was no hint in an expression caught between curiosity and a determination not to appear ungrateful. In my innocence I had no such diplomacy.

'Look,' I shouted pointing at the plate – and Tommy did – 'Kit-e-Kat sandwiches.' Just by that Tommy noticed the empty tin on the sideboard. He looked at me. He looked at my grandmother. And, as though on cue, 'Ma' re-emerged into the society from under the settee. She was licking her whiskers.

Tommy's face paled. Flustered by the day's events my grandmother stammered but, cute enough, opted not to deny serving cat food. Tommy stared at 'Ma'. His face went from red to white to green.

'Mrs Toner I'll just head on. I better fix that windie at the back. It might blow in. I'm away so I am. Away. No bother. Thanks. Sure sit down and take the weight off your feet. I'm away now. Goodnight. Goodnight. Goodnight.' He was gone, down the hall and away.

The door, unbalanced by the bomb, creaked closed behind him.

It would have been silent had it not been for a hymn floating out of the television. 'All things bright and beautiful, all creatures great and small.'

I looked at the adults, colour was rising in my grandmother's cheeks. They looked at the cat, for her part looking strangely smug. The whole room erupted into laughter, my grandfather doubling over and my grandmother holding on to the table to steady herself. An uncle patted me on the head as if congratulating me.

When the laughter subsided, my grandmother picked off a portion of the corned beef from the plate abandoned by Tommy and threw it on to the ground for the cat. 'Ma' sniffed cautiously, blinked twice, turned and hopped on to my grandfather's lap. She had, it seemed, one thing in common with Tommy. Neither liked corned beef.

Dereliction

We got off the number nine bus. At first, it was as it had been. Then, reaching the fork into our part of the street, I hardly recognised anything. Eyes and mind clashed. The hedges were unkempt, there were splintered gaps in fences, there were no people. Broken glass, bricks and stones were strewn on the pavement and across the roadway. Our game there had been 'cribbie', throwing a ball in an attempt to bounce it off the opposite kerb. The thought came to me that, with all the glass, any ball would soon be punctured. Where we had played in the field, becoming adventurers and explorers, I could make out a homemade wooden cross, decaying flowers or wreaths just visible around its base. It was cool, a Sunday afternoon for my father was off work. I do not remember the month. It had rained. A moist greyness infused everything.

We stopped before our home, the house where we had lived. The lawn my father had cut neat as a bowling green was tangled with long yellow grass, mare's-tail and chickweed. The cherry tree was straggly, unpruned, and around the borders rose bushes were topped by rotted petals. I looked at the gates. A fleck of rust showed through the dent where I had crashed my bicycle.

'We'll go in, in a minute,' my father said.

We walked further up the hill, beyond the bend. It was worse. All the houses on the left backing onto Springmartin were not only derelict but destroyed. Stained and torn curtains wafted through broken glass and frames. Doors were hanging off their hinges. Nothing of value was left. Breeze blocks covered the windows and doors of a couple of houses, adding to the overwhelming sense of greyness. But for a few crows and their cawing, it was deserted and silent. I looked at the house where the American family had lived. Every pane was broken. They were from Belfast, of course, returning when the father got out of the army. It was their dream home. He brought with him a trunk of G.I. uniforms. We laughed putting them on, trying to roll up the sleeves until our arms fitted.

My father was moving more cautiously now, as though, I thought, trying not to disturb the birds. They might inform on our presence. He pointed to some holes in the brickwork, which, he said, had been made by bullets.

The blocks overlooking from Springmartin, peppered with bullet holes, were also deserted. As they offered such a vantage point over the area, the IRA in Ballymurphy and New Barnsley had emptied rounds into them and the line of houses along the ridge that stretched down to the main road. My father shook his head.

As we walked back around, one of a handful of remaining neighbours approached.

'I saw you passing, Jim,' he said. 'Is there any word?'

'None,' was the reply.

My father sort of shrugged and winced at the same time, flattening his palms to indicate nothing. He was in a group trying to secure some compensation. Because the houses had not been burnt, were still 'structurally intact' as officials put it, the insurance companies were refusing to pay. From their London offices, they argued that the street was still habitable. The residents had no lawyers, no money, no hope. Like the others, my parents continued to pay their mortgages to avoid defaulting on bank loans. Still, my father and the rest of their small committee continued to press their case wherever they could get a hearing. In the Belfast of the early seventies, chaotic, murderous and unstable, no one wanted to listen.

Many residents simply disappeared. Neighbouring families, one Protestant and the other Catholic, seemingly boarded a plane for Canada, where they moved to neighbouring homes. At least one couple went to Scotland. Others headed to the Republic. During holidays, years later, my parents met a woman they knew walking along the main street in Arklow. It turned out that in the immediate aftermath of the shooting and internment, three or four families from the street got on a train and went to Wicklow, County Wicklow, as far south as their money could take them. People there welcomed the refugees, setting them up in houses, finding jobs for the husbands at a big chemical plant near the town.

The Housing Executive offered my parents accommodation in the new town of Craigavon. Some thirty miles from Belfast, between Portadown and Lurgan, it was designed as the new model for communities living in harmony.

'Craigavon?' My father laughed at the idea.

Some of our neighbours found almost completed developments in west Belfast and squatted there rent-free. Volunteers keen to help hooked up water mains and electricity supplies. Eventually agreement was reached with the builders and arrangements were regularised. They encouraged my parents to go there, but my mother, unnerved by her experiences, could not accept more uncertainty.

The majority of them scattered across Belfast, most returning to their home districts. Through word of mouth, enough to form an ad hoc committee were located.

'You were right to get out, Jim,' said the neighbour. 'I'd be away myself if I could find somewhere. You can't cross the door here at night now.'

My father commiserated, said he would keep in touch 'if there was any word'.

He and I walked up our drive and climbed the steps. The key would not open the front door. My father tried again, taking it out, double-checking he had brought the right key. He stared at it as if it had turned traitor. Through the opaque glass panel at the side of the door, we saw movement inside. A young woman opened the door.

'Are you the owner?' she asked my father.

She invited us in and we walked up the hall, me looking at all the scuffs to the perfect varnished wooden tiles laid by my parents. About the same age, her husband was in the back room. It looked like they were using boxes as seats. A record player was on the floor and some infant items. A toddler was careering around the floor, giggling, in some sort of a baby walker. The man had a second baby in his arms.

There was talk, although to me what they were saying was background noise. I searched for something familiar in what I was seeing, trying in my mind to place ourselves back there, struggling to take in the change. It was impossible. I had watched the moon landing in this room. Now there was no television. Table and chairs were gone, there was no couch and there were none of my mother's vases, which seemed to have flowers all year round. On the walls you could see lighter outlines where our pictures had hung. There was no light in the Sacred Heart lamp socket. In the grate where my father rolled up newspapers to light the coal and turf, there was a tiny electric fire, its glowing bars projecting a little heat.

Slowly I picked up some of what was being said.

They apologised for changing the lock, they wanted to come and go safely. They too had been put out of their home somewhere along the boundary line in north Belfast. They told him their names. My father did not say much. I think he too might have been trying to make sense of it all. They asked if he wished to look around, he said he did not. The baby woke crying for a bottle. When we left, my father shook their hands and told them not to worry. I thought I saw the woman wipe a tear from her eye.

We stood in the middle of the street and looked back.

'Well, that's it,' said my father. He let out a sigh as though finally coming to terms with all that had taken place. 'There's no living here now anyway. We'll not be back so we won't.'

I could hear him rehearse the words he would say to my mother. There was now the merest hint of a tear in his eye.

I was becoming angry for seeing others in our space, for the helplessness and for the hurt to my parents. I blurted out what I was thinking: 'Who are they? What are they doing in our house? Why did you not tell them to leave?'

He looked at me, gently, and then gestured for me to look around the all-but-deserted street.

'If those people think this is safer and better, then where they've come from must be really bad, mustn't it? There's no way we'll be putting them out. It was wrong when it was done to us and it would be wrong for us to do it to them, wouldn't it?'

The way he put the questions, I could only agree. Until that day I had imagined that somehow things would be waved back as they had been, that all would be fixed, healed, magic. I knew now this would never happen. It was no longer our home.

We walked back down the street. I stared straight ahead, not looking at the priest's house, the cross on the slope of the field, the mountain or the stream, though I heard its trickle. It started to rain, softly sweeping down from Divis. The number nine bus arrived. We got on and sat, me nearest the window. I did not look behind at the street that had once been home. Neither, I noticed, did my father. We moved off. We moved on.

Snow

Snow fell that Sunday night. We peered from the windows willing it to lie. A sudden flurry turned into a skiff and then the big white flakes came swirling out of a purple-black sky.

We had been put out of our home and were living in a house on the front of the Springfield Road not far from the barracks. It was given to us by a friend of my mother who had heard of our predicament, sleeping on the floors, settees and spare rooms of family and friends. Harry, a prematurely early retired teacher, would have given us the house for nothing just to ensure it was occupied. My mother insisted on paying rent, handed weekly to his aunt because Harry took a drink. A gentle soul, sometimes he would call apologetically at the door and then have a cup of tea, chatting to my father, ensuring he would go to the aunt's house, where he lived entirely steady, not smelling of alcohol. He was very quiet, patient by nature and extremely polite even when slightly slurring his words.

The house was on Hughes' Terrace, a long three-storey line stretching up towards the bakery. It was closer to my school than Springfield Park, so I stayed all week with my parents. We lived there for almost two years until we finally received a Housing Executive rental closer to my father's new job. When he left Mackie's after thirty-two years pushing, pulling and coaxing machines, the firm presented him with a fountain pen.

Rooms in the temporary accommodation were dark, not decorated since Harry's parents had died. Even during the day, it was shadowy. The wiring was such that there were limited light fittings and plug points. My mother and father painted the rooms we used most with whites and magnolias, and they got my uncle to install a fluorescent light in the kitchen, these the only nods to modernity. There was no phone, although my grandmother's house was much closer.

I hated Harry's house, never had any confidence in its gloomy recesses, high ceilings or top rooms where furniture was shrouded in sheets. A flight of stairs soared directly from the hall. Not long after we had moved in, my father was on a night shift and during particularly heavy gunfire, my mother determined she and I should go downstairs. She went first with blankets. I followed. Seeing tracer fire whizz past the glass of the front door I found myself unable to move, fear-fixed, drowning. After minutes, it may have been seconds, I put one foot in front of the other, making it to the relative security of the downstairs back room.

This Sunday night, the last in January 1972, the adults were packed into that room. Aside from my parents, Harry was there, the next-door neighbours and Eileen, a family friend who lived around the corner. I came in to tell them about the snow. They were not interested. The radio was on RTÉ, the Republic's broadcaster, a series of newsflashes coming through. Periodically there would be a flurry of activity when my father would tweak the dial in a flustered attempt to retrieve a lost signal.

Outside, no cars moved. It was the closest thing Belfast could get to a blizzard. In no time at all several inches were lying. Friends were starting to throw snowballs. It was about half past seven. I asked if I could go out. I fully expected a fuss, given that I had to be in school the following day. My mother told me to be sure to wear a coat. Duffel on and away I went leaving them tied to the radio.

Snow, it seemed, was falling all over the city. I looked up and a big flake settled on my cheek. There were shouts and cheers. I grabbed a crunchy handful, compacted it into a big powdery ball and entered the fray. About half a dozen of us were whirling wild, every man for himself. Normally we clodded only stones. Snow was a rare innocence, pure somehow. When we had lived up towards Divis we had it each year, once at Christmas. Down in the city it never seemed to snow and being able to take aim at friends in our own streets seemed hardly believable.

Thud. A snowball hit me right in the ear – wet, watery, cold and dulling sound even more. More youngsters were joining in, coming from the street around the corner, drawn by our yells. Most we knew, at least to see, yet, without organisation and almost telepathically, sides formed. We held our line, they held their line and we pelted each other, celebrating the strikes, lamenting near misses. Still snow fell.

After about half an hour, my hands were freezing, my coat wringing and my hair wet from snow and sweat. I pushed at the front door and went inside to warm my hands. The adults had not moved. I noticed that, unusually, there were as yet no teacups or biscuits on the table. Moreover, my mother scarcely noticed the puddle at my shoes, the black leather leaching white. No one asked about the snow.

I edged near to the fire, my hands quickly pained by the heat. The sting slowly throbbing just in my fingertips, I listened to snippets of conversation. Seven people, I heard, had been killed by soldiers in Derry. The Parachute Regiment, Civil Rights, Bernadette, John Hume and Ivan Cooper, all were mentioned. I could tell the adults were as agitated by the news as I was by the snow. I thought of my grandmother's cats when a thunderstorm was approaching. There was a knock at the door and I went out to the hall. A friend wanted me back out, a snowball hit the lintel above, showering us, and I was back in the battle.

After a further fifteen minutes, the pattern was repeated. Anticipation of the pain made it no easier. This time I heard the music on RTÉ halt abruptly and an announcer's soothing, seductive, soft Dublin brogue: 'We interrupt this programme for a newsflash and go over to the newsroom.'

The next voice was more hurried. 'Good evening. At least nine people have been shot dead by British soldiers in Derry. They were attending a Civil Rights march, which had been banned by the northern authorities. The shooting happened in the Bogside area around Rossville Flats. Eyewitnesses say members of the Parachute Regiment opened fire and that those killed were unarmed. We will bring you more details in our next news bulletin at nine o'clock. We return now to our regular programming.'

The music that followed seemed ill-fitting.

'At least nine,' my father said. The sense of disbelief was great.

'They said they had no guns,' said Eileen.

Harry shook his head. 'It was the Paras.'

'They've murdered them, that's what they've done,' said the man who lived next door.

I slipped out. The snow was so thick now you had to strain your eyes to focus on individual flakes. Youngsters from the other street were grey outlines behind the dapples of snow, backlit from the window of the shop up on the corner. We still could not resist loosing a spontaneous snowball when a target came close enough, but now we were sliding down the wide pavement and even the middle of the road, with a foot in front, toes pointed, and a foot behind to act as a brake.

On the edge of the road four or five kids were building a snowman, heaving and straining together to roll a body several feet high. I could see my breath in front of my face and cupped my hands around my mouth trying to heat them. Not a car was on the road, not an adult was outside. No sounds save our own penetrated the deadness of the snow.

I went back inside. The news came on RTÉ. This time the newsreader said eleven people had been killed. Other than that, the story as told sounded similar, except this time a reporter in Derry was delivering the news. His tone was sharp, different from the usual measure. He said that the toll might yet rise. Eileen's eyes brimmed glassy. My mother seemed as though she might cry as well. Everything felt uneasy.

Outside again, the snowman was bigger and now had a head in position. Someone had produced a rotten potato for a nose and two lumps of coal made up the eyes. A mouth seemed to have been carved out, possibly with the coal, giving it an expression more scary than jolly. Three girls shrieked when they were targeted by a broadside of snowballs as they left the shop. Cold and time were against us. I arranged to meet one of my classmates at the corner in the morning to go to school.

The last news I heard that night said thirteen men had been killed in Derry. The way the numbers climbed unevenly that evening was the most memorable detail. The adults were still listening to RTÉ. When the news came on the television, it was the BBC and they shouted some remarks. There were grainy pictures of soldiers running, men spreadeagled against a wall, an army 'pig' driving over some waste ground and then a priest with a bloody handkerchief chasing away a soldier as others behind carried a flopping body. This image froze the room. The priest told of innocent people shot as they ran away. An officer said his men were fired upon. Harry said, 'He's lying.' My father nodded. 'That's it,' he said. My mother made tea.

My father was on an early shift. He would be leaving the house by six. Sometime around eleven o'clock Harry, Eileen and the neighbours left, remarking at the depth and suddenness of the blizzard. The brightness compensated for the lack of street lights. I went to bed. From below the sheets, all cold and shivery, I looked out the window where the occasional big flake would tap soft as a kitten's paws.

Snow was still falling, in broad curling spirals on the rooftops and, down the road, on the barracks, on its sand-bags, corrugated metal and barbed wire. I imagined it deep in the street where we used to live, now full of houses with breeze-blocked windows, and wondered if it was falling in Derry where all those had fallen and whether it melted sticky into the blood. Already outside it was covering our tracks from earlier and making all appear cleansed.

My mother got me up for school. The first thing I did was look out the window. Little curtains of ice laced the corners of the pane. The snow was deep. The snowman, almost opposite our house, leered back at me. I hopped out of the warmth of the bed. The radio was on in the background. My mother would comment occasionally. 'Awful, awful,' she said. She told me she was unsure if I should go to school. 'There will be trouble,' she said.

The lure of the snow was magnetic.

'I have to go in,' I said. 'I can't miss class today and I have to meet Dessie.'

I was convincing. My mother had to leave shortly for her own work. I could see her weighing things. Reluctantly, she agreed. There was a frantic search for homework and schoolbag, rulers and pens. My coat was dry and cosy from having been put on a chair in front of the fire. Off I went, my mother heading one way and me up to the corner where Dessie was already waiting, waving outside the shop. His younger brother was with him.

Our usual route was normally straightforward; not this day. We took the odd slide, pushed each other for fun and threw a random snowball. There was little to aim at and we found ourselves hurrying. The streets were quiet. We reached the open ground once dominated by brick kilns, the 'brickfields' or the 'brickie' we called it. Cleared now for new houses, work had not started, so it was open ground. Puddles, concrete slabs, muck and stones were gone, the snow uncorrupting all. In the corner furthest from us, a lorry had been set on fire. Set in the snowscape, the bright red of the flames and rubber-black smoke were rich, the only colours, vibrant and saturated. There was a crumpled thud as the petrol tank went up. Flames spat out. We were momentarily mesmerised. The gunfire, a short automatic burst, was startling. All three of us threw ourselves face first into the snow. There was the crack of a pistol next and we heard the whizz of a bullet. We were not being fired at, but the shooting was nearby, uncomfortable. The ground felt safe. We made ourselves small and crawled thirty yards on our bellies so quickly towards the exit from the waste ground we hardly became wet. There we had the cover of houses. We stood up, wiped the snow off, laughed and continued on our way.

School was just at the top of the street. We threw snowballs in a playground not a quarter full. The first bell went. Grudgingly we went to our class, a temporary mobile room behind the main school block. Out of a class of thirty-four, seven of us were in class. The teacher, Mr Mulvenna, seemed surprised we were there at all. He handed us big sheets of paper and marker pens.

'Draw what happened in Derry yesterday,' he said. He left us alone in the classroom, damp and chilled from the weekend, plodding off through a drift to join his colleagues inside where they presumably were debating all that had taken place. Ordinarily on a Monday morning, the chance to draw, to avoid writing and rote arithmetic tables, would have been an incredible departure. This was no ordinary day.

We drew armoured cars and soldiers. Periodically we would look out at the snow and wish away the hours until lunch when we could get back to the playground.

Then it happened. The low cloud wisped away to reveal skies leaden, not purple like the previous night. The first big japs of rain hit the window. 'It'll turn to snow,' said one of the other lads. It did not and the change in temperature was obvious. The rain became steadily heavier and after forty-five minutes we could see dirty grey gaps in the snow. Dismayed, our strokes on our pages became bolder. Red-flash firing came from the guns, the soldiers' berets were red and the figures of people on the ground were bleeding hot, almost black-red like the smoke and flames from the lorry.

It must have been three hours. Master Mulvenna came back, a drip on his nose from the rain. He took a cursory look at our handiwork. 'Terrible, terrible,' he said. 'That's what happened all right.' Then he told us we were to be allowed home at lunchtime because the school would be closing for three days until after the funerals. 'There might be trouble,' he said. The lunch bell rang. We went out.

We ran in vain, looking for some spot of banked snow. It was gone, all gone, melted by the rain washing it from the rooftops and into gutters, and turning the football field we shared with the secondary school to waterlogged mud. It had melted across the city and was now patchy, even on the higher slopes of the mountain. On the way home, we had to jump over the water running down drains. The snowman outside our house was gone as well. Others had pushed it over and a passing lorry left it an oily sludge pile. One of the coaly eyes had been ground into the tarmac; the other was intact on top of the sludge. Crows and pigeons had made off with the potato. All was grey and the world we had set out in that morning had changed, changed with an outright certainty.

Homecoming

It was planned for the Easter holidays. We went into Belfast by bus, me expecting to go to the shops. Instead, we walked up a hill, into an imposing building, its overpowering odour of disinfectant and carbolic soap. The next thing I knew a doctor in a white coat shoved a wooden lollipop stick into my mouth, telling me to say 'aaah'.

'They'll have to come out,' he told my mother, booking me in for the following week.

After a run of throat and ear infections, the solution was apparently to remove my tonsils.

All week they kept it light, my parents. The day came around and they broke it to me that I would have to remain in hospital that night. It was the first time I had been away from family.

I have no recollection of preparations for the tonsillectomy or even arrival at the hospital that morning. My only impression is of a light-green, shiny-tiled theatre and a nurse and doctor in full scrubs. I fought against the rubber mask descending from the ceiling and, ignoring an instruction to breathe deeply, I lost focus to a rectangle of impossibly bright light above.

A nurse patted my face telling me it was all over, that I was all right, that I could come round. Still woozy, I immediately vomited bile and blood. The nurse matter-of-factly and belatedly placed a cardboard spittoon under my chin. The smell reminded me of the gas. I vomited again. I realised I was in some sort of side room just as a porter, accompanied by the nurse, began to wheel me along corridors. We went to a minor surgery ward in a lift with latticed iron gates. As it ascended to the third floor, it clanked, whirred and shuddered so that, in that moment, my fear of what had been done to my throat was replaced by a scary sensation of falling. It stopped. The porter clanked back the gates and wheeled me out directly into the ward, where they helped me into a bed. The sheets were cold and starchy. I threw up again, this time into the cardboard. I slept.

When I woke, my father was sitting at the end of the bed. He had a pass out of work. I was lying, my back propped up by a big stiff pillow. He put a hand on my forehead. There was no temperature. The smell of stale oil on his overalls felt familiar, comforting. When I tried to speak, it was as if nettles had bloomed in my throat.

'Don't talk son. Is it sore?'

I gave up trying to speak and rose to spit more blood into the cardboard. He held the spittoon. 'You'll be home in a few days.'

A few days? I had thought perhaps an overnight stay.

For the first time I looked around the ward. There were about a dozen beds on either side, leading from the doors down to a window as tall as my grandmother's house. Almost all of the beds were occupied. Mine was midway along. A few tables, trestles similar to those in our school dinner hall, stretched down the centre of the ward.

A nurse rang a hand bell. The doors swung open, visiting time. Other parents arrived, mainly mothers, younger children in tow. My mother came in, relieved having exchanged a darted glance with my father that told her all she needed to know. She smiled at me, keeping it bright, producing from her bag a sheaf of comics. My head stayed on the pillow. Movement stoked the fire in my throat. My mother put her hand on my head. I smelled her perfume, her palm, soft, warm, like home.

'Is it sore?'

My father answered for me.

'It is, a wee bit. He can't talk. I told him he'll be here only a couple of nights. How many comics do you have there?'

I glanced towards the glossy covers, hardly interested.

Looking up and down the ward, I could see that perhaps half a dozen others seemed to be in the same position as me. All had doleful expressions and cardboard spittoons nearby. The lad in the bed next to me, towards the door, had his back to us. In the opposite direction, another boy, a redhead, was propped up on his pillow, his mother and younger sister, also a redhead, chattering around his bedside. Clearly on the mend, a couple ran up and down the ward in pyjamas and slippers. My mother held up the comic on my chest and turned a couple of pages. There were so many distractions it was impossible to concentrate on the words.

The hand bell rang again in the corridor. Nurses emerged, exchanging pleasantries with the parents, tidying away bits and bobs from bedside tables and making a show of fussing. Visiting time was over. My parents were neither first nor last to leave, promising they would return that evening. They did. The seven o'clock visit went much the same. The lad in the next bed was sleeping. For him there were no visitors. On the other side, the whole family was there; mother, father, the little sister and two older brothers. I heard his name mentioned, Sean. For me there were more comics, a puzzle book, still no possibility of speaking and my mother and father doing all the talking before a nurse rang the bell. Lights were switched out at half past nine, much earlier than my usual bedtime at home. I lay awake, twitching at every sound in the corridors and the occasional clashes and clanks from the lift. Exhausted, I drifted to a deep anaesthetic-aided sleep.

The hospital wakened with the noise of the lift, trolleys and plates. Nibbling a piece of dry toast, I imagined how my father had cut a rose bush with secateurs. Afterwards, drinking some lukewarm milk was soothing. Much later in the morning, nurses chased the more lively patients to bed and the consultant who had removed my tonsils processed down the ward with a matron as stiff as her apron and hat. They were followed by a panic of fresh-faced medical students, all stethoscopes and teeth, and, even to me, clearly eager to impress.

They stopped at the bed next to me where the lad had hardly moved all morning, his big saucer-like eyes staring ahead while others at the tables had played games – ludo, draughts and snakes and ladders, brought out of tatty-edged boxes.

Approaching his bed, the consultant became gentle.

'Well sir, how are we doing today?'

His voice was soft yet carried authority.

I did not hear any reply.

'Let's take a little look and see how you are coming along.'

The matron instructed two nurses with a look and they

moved in a practised way to pull curtains around the bed. Because the medical students, five of them, were trying to crowd into the cubicle, the curtain was partially open. I noticed the matron raise a stern eyebrow at one student who encroached too far. He started and took a full step back. I could not see but heard the consultant clearly.

'Oh, that looks much better. It's not sore any more is it, Martin?'

I heard nothing by way of response.

'We'll be getting you home soon.'

Then his voice hardened. 'Let's make sure we keep it clean matron, but that looks much better. Two or three more days maybe. You can let the family know.'

A nurse and the medical students scribbled frantically on clipboards.

On the other side, Sean, like me, was leafing through a comic. We managed faint grins of acknowledgement. Neither of us tried to speak. We had both been listening to the examination.

'Right Mr Kelters, how are we doing today?'

It was the first time any adult had called me mister. I was secretly pleased. Again, he asked me to croak out an 'aaah', while holding my tongue down with a wooden spatula that was just as quickly discarded into a bag held by one of the nurses.

'Coming along nicely. You'll be home in no time.'

Off went the procession, stopping briefly at Sean's bed for much the same drill before continuing down the ward.

That afternoon when the visiting bell rang, my grandparents came in, my grandmother fretting right away. 'Is it sore? Can you speak? It must be awful?'

I attempted a reassuring smile.

'Och, he's a big boy now. That'll not be sore for him.' My grandfather was much more functional. I could not decide which approach I preferred. More comics were produced along with some fizzy bottle that promised to aid recovery. Some of the comics, I noticed, were the same as those brought in the day before. I took a sip of the glucose drink.

Sean's mother was there again, but again Martin had no visitors. I caught his eye briefly as he watched my grandparents. He quickly looked away.

'This is the same ward all right,' my grandfather said. 'There were a lot more people in it then.'

Putting my fingers into the deep depression, knobbly smooth in his left arm was an early memory. I knew the story. It was a wound inflicted half a century earlier by police. Four fired. One bullet missed, one cut his tie in half and one went clean through the back of his shirt without hitting him. The rifle round that struck was a snub-nosed dum-dum. It smashed through flesh and sinew near the muscle. He was seventeen. It was during a curfew and he was kneeling over a fatally injured man at Millfield. Seven men were thrown into a meat wagon that took them away. My grandfather was the only one to live. He spent six months in the hospital where they saved his arm. While he was there, with the complicity of staff in the ward, beds and patients were shifted daily like a three-cup trick to allow a bandaged IRA man to escape custody.

My grandfather's eyes drifted away down the ward, visiting 1921.

'Would you like some ice cream?'

My grandmother brought us to the present. It sounded soothing, like it might put out the fire.

'I'll get your mummy to bring some tonight.'

Hope receded.

They chatted. I listened. The bell rang and they left.

Before teatime, a nurse with a bandage set pulled the curtains around Martin's bed.

My grandmother was good to her word and that evening my mother brought ice cream. It was Italian, smoother than the mass-produced local kind that arrived in little card boxes. My father had carried it in a tub from Fusco's shop on the front of the Falls. Tentative spoonfuls slid down, numbing in the hackles at the back of my throat.

Sean's bedside was packed. No one was with Martin.

'Would you like some?'

Martin started. He had been caught staring. My mother did not wait for a reply. She fetched a clean bowl and spoon from the stack on a table where they had been left for breakfast, filled it from the carton and brought it to Martin. He nodded thanks, greedily scraping the bowl. He managed to smile back at my mother.

My father held his hand out to me.

'Come on down the ward and see what you can see.'

He wanted to get me out of bed. Standing up for the first time, I was a little light-headed. My father placed his hand on my shoulder to guide me down the ward to the window.

The hospital, the Mater Infirmorum, was on the Crumlin Road towards the north of the city. A more natural choice of location for me would have been the Royal Belfast Hospital for Sick Children around the corner from my grandmother's house, but I think I was sent where our family doctor knew the surgeon. Known to all as the Mater, it was a red-brick building that, from the outside, looked something like a Victorian folly. Our ward's window was flanked by two turrets topped with faux battlements. Founded by nuns, the hospital looked across to the familiar spires of St Peter's and Divis Tower. Directly on the far side of the Crumlin Road was the Shankill district. 'It was a great shopping road,' I had heard my grandmother say, but we no longer ventured there. The veins of streets that once linked the roads had been cauterised by a series of makeshift barricades, army checkpoints and no-man's lands of derelict houses. Culturally conflicting, all that united them now was poverty, slums and fierce pride.

My father pointed out the 'Hammer' and the 'Nick', telling me about the decent men he worked with who came from those districts. It was still bright. He told me about the courthouse up the road. Even though I pressed my nose to the window, I could not see it. My father told me there was a tunnel from it under the road to the prison next to the hospital. 'They're both busy now,' my father said. I looked in vain for any undulation to betray the tunnel in the road. There were more buses than cars. I wondered what would happen if they fell into the tunnel.

My father sensed me straining to look for the fields below Divis where I had played.

'You'll be home soon.'

He meant the house they were renting. He steered me back down the ward to my bed.

My mother had tidied away the comics. Some were on

Martin's bed and he had one opened, studying it. The bell rang. Martin exchanged a soft smile with my mother. They said their goodbyes, my parents chatting to Sean's mother and father as they left the ward.

Sean smiled at me. I gestured at a comic. He held out his hands as if to play catch and I threw one to him. He grinned. I looked at Martin. He had a trace of a smile.

'Thank you.'

It was the first time I had heard his voice, different to the harsh twang of Belfast, a lilt, a yielding quality. I nodded okay. Lights were turned off at the same time that night.

I woke to the sound of crying. Three or four kids started it off. I may have been one of them. In minutes, it seemed as if the entire ward had joined a choral howl. It spread to other wards. No nurses appeared. We cried ourselves out, fell asleep, exhausted, on pillows wetted by tears. In the morning, we eyed the ward through bleary eyes, looking at each other sheepishly, avoiding each other's gaze. I noticed Martin's eyes were not red like the rest of us.

The doctors' round that morning followed the pattern of the previous day, although this time no curtains were drawn around Martin's bed. Through the crowd I glimpsed the doctor examine a dressing on his side. Martin remained quiet. The consultant was gentle with him.

'You are nearly there, Martin. It won't be long. To-morrow maybe.'

They arrived at my bed. He depressed my tongue again and made me say 'aaah'. This time when he asked me how I was doing, I hacked out that I was okay. The sound of my voice, however husky, surprised me. They swept on, the junior doctors tripping over themselves.

That morning Sean and I played ludo at the table. We held up the dice to Martin and he joined us. A nurse brought us three glasses of milk. Nervous with each other at first, we soon laughed as the numbers turned. Sean and I were much at the same stage when it came to finding our voices. It was a small start, but we managed to croak out our counts as we stepped our markers around the board. Martin could speak, but he was less vocal than either of us. During the third or fourth game, Sean pointed at him.

'What's wrong?'

Martin shrunk. He retreated into himself. He shook his head.

'I'm all right.'

The one of us who had a voice did not want to use it and we were quiet for a while until sucked back into the game.

My mother got out of work early and was back that afternoon; more ice cream shared with Martin. Sean's mother brought him a full bottle of brown lemonade. Small wonder everyone in the ward ran around for an hour after visiting time. A football appeared and disappeared when it was kicked through the doors at the far end and into the open lift as its gate slammed closed.

That evening we heard a burst of gunfire. It was hard to tell where, not that far away, perhaps across the barricades. I worried about my father and mother, but they had not heard the shots and poured in with the others at the sound of the bell. By now, my mother had established she had once worked with Sean's aunt. The city was like that then; a dewy hawthorn hedge web where touching one point of tension blinked elsewhere. Sean's parents talked with mine and Martin's bedside was still empty. My mother had brought him more ice cream and, as well, gave him sweets that I still could not eat. For the first time I could speak to my parents.

'When do I go home?'

'Soon son. Soon. The doctors might tell us tomorrow.'

My mother had also brought some comics for Martin. While my father chatted with me, she sat and read to Martin. My father walked me down to the window again and got me to point out places to him, making me use my voice more. As I returned, I saw my mother talking to Martin, then giving him a hug. He nestled his head into her shoulder. Seeing us, she shook her head with a glassy make-no-mention look.

When a nurse rang the bell, my mother was still talking quietly to Martin. She gave him another hug and that night my parents were last to leave the ward, saying their goodbyes to Sean, Martin and me.

The crying started again. It woke me; it must have been around three in the morning. I think it might have begun in a neighbouring ward. It spread along our ward like a contagion. I found myself crying uncontrollably, bawling into my pillow to stifle the noise, crying for the pain, for being away from my parents, for losing our home. I drifted off to sleep finally as rays of dawn streaked through the window.

I woke with the clatter of the lift gate. A nurse wheeled a trolley with the usual array of hot food plates and cereal. More hungry than previously, I had scrambled egg, a slice of toast and milk. Sean was eating, so was Martin, his eyes swollen, bloated, red. After breakfast, we played ludo again. We could speak more but were somehow more muted, fatigued and embarrassed by the previous night's tears.

The consultant and his entourage arrived and brushed down the ward. No curtains were pulled this time. I heard the doctor speaking, his voice soothing.

'Well Martin, do you think you are well enough to leave us?'

Martin must have said yes.

'So do I young man. So do I. You'll be glad to see the back of us after all these weeks won't you?'

I heard Martin say, 'Thank you doctor.'

'Sister, you'll make the arrangements.'

'Yes Mr Caldwell.' She made a phone sign – thumb to ear, finger to mouth – to one of the nurses, shooing her from the ward.

Sean and myself were examined quickly. We had lunch, beans on toast. Afterwards, the ball appeared again. It was thrown from bed to bed, most dancing on top of their sheets, whooping when someone dropped the ball. A nurse took it away after we knocked over half a tinny pitcher of water. She cleaned it up, telling us sternly to be quiet and rest for a while.

I dozed, worn from recovery and the previous night's lack of sleep. When I woke, the curtains were again around Martin's bed. A nurse opened them and a woman was sitting there alongside him. His pyjamas were gone and at first I struggled to recognise him. He was wearing outside clothes: shoes, trousers, a shirt and pullover.

'Say bye-bye,' the woman said. She had the same country accent as Martin.

He went to Sean's bed and said goodbye. Then he came to me.

'Do you want the comics back?'

'No, I've read them. You take them.'

He seemed pleased. He leaned close to me.

'Tell your mummy I said thanks.'

It was the most I had heard him say.

'For the ice cream?'

'For everything.'

Colour rising in his cheeks, the nurses hugged him. The woman picked up a small case from the bed and took Martin's hand.

'Time now, Martin. I'll take you home.'

He waved a hesitant wave as off they went.

Twenty minutes later the bell rang and my mother came in. She had taken a half day off work. She noticed immediately that Martin was gone.

'He went with his mummy,' I told her. The words were coming more easily.

She looked at me. I could tell she was weighing up what to say.

'Seamus, that must have been his aunt. His mummy and daddy were in a car crash a few weeks ago.'

'He said to thank you. What did you say to him?'

'I told him they're in heaven now and they'll always be watching over him.'

I tried to understand.

'He only needed a hug son, that's all. Poor wee soul. He just needed a hug.'

She was back later with my father.

That night the crying woke me again. This time I did

not join in. I thought of Martin, his mother and father. I slept. His bed was occupied the next day by another lad wheeled in, wan-faced, the spittoon on his chest. Sean and I quietly gloated. In a while the consultant came. He cleared the pair of us to leave.

That afternoon my mother arrived with my clothes. It felt good to discard pyjamas and put on shoes. My mother prompted me to thank the nurses and give them a small box of chocolates. I stepped forward, embarrassed. Sean and I shook hands a little formally. We were self-conscious. I walked shakily to the elevator and the gates clanked shut. This time I was too relieved to be nervous. The light of the fine spring sunshine made my eyes flicker. My mother had put my father's scarf around my mouth for protection from germs. Even so, free from the heat and disinfectant I gasped at the cooler air. It hurt slightly. She led me down through the city streets and round by Peter's Hill, past Brown Square and Millfield, where my grandfather had been shot so many years before.

My mother asked if I would like to stop for ice cream. I thought of Martin again going back to a cold house, no mother or father. A shiver ran up my spine. I squeezed her hand tighter.

'No thanks. I want to go home.'

Lesson

He was a bully, intimidating youngsters through violence, threat and the temper of one who knew that, whatever he did, he had absolute authority. Paddy Fitzsimmons was the principal during most of the years I was at the school, both the new building at the top of Beechmount and the old two-storey red-brick in the square. It was attended by my father and my mother's brothers forty years earlier. 'Fitzy', as he was known behind his back by colleagues and pupils alike, had taught my father in the thirties.

Because I knew the area, periodically with another boy I was sent up the entry by the barracks then across the main Springfield Road to Harry Greenwood's shop. He was a genial man of an eclectic taste reflected in the stock laid out higgledy-piggledy on his shelves. Baked beans sat alongside women's stockings, sewing machine oil below boiled sweets. My grandmother went there to purchase snuff. On some Friday afternoons, Miss Ware, my first teacher, would send us to buy more than thirty 'Lucky Bags'. Paid for from her own pennies, these she would distribute to the entire class and we would pour out all sorts of plastic novelties on our desks, everyone oohing and aahing, and she smiling all the time just for seeing the joy. When we made the trip to Greenwood's for Paddy Fitzsimmons, it was not to get lucky bags. Instead it was to buy canes, long bamboo canes as boney-cold as himself. He wore them out regularly.

When I was seven, after we had gone to the new building, my class was close to Fitzy's office. He threw open the door, accusing us of making too much noise. The class went silent. Closest to him, I was pulled out. He lashed down with a cane; six times on each hand, not pretend slaps, not measured. The cane swished down from behind his head, cutting stripes across each palm. I went back to my classroom, tears of real pain turning everything a watery blur. My teacher, Mrs Ramsey, a kindly woman, was visibly shocked. She let me sit in the corner, hands nursed into my pullover, the streaks on my face drying.

The following day my mother went to the school to complain. She discovered him kicking a child on the ground around the playground. Her words were sharp. She threatened to report him to the parish priest. Paddy Fitzsimmons never hit me again, although I witnessed his brutality to others on several occasions. Physical punishment was by no means uncommon in the school, but most other teachers used it reluctantly. Fitzy's cruelty was in real contrast to the decency of the others who shepherded us through those times. It was not an easy job, the work taken on by Jimmy Prentice and Micky Barr. They were men who led by calm and strong example. Never did I see either of them genuinely lose their temper with any of us though, it has to be said, there was ample justification.

We were changing, becoming wild because of what was going on outside and sometimes inside the school gates.

The atmosphere between people and soldiers had shifted.

A big boundary of Falls streets below the Springfield junction was curfewed during house-to-house raids for guns. Attempting to reason with an armoured car, an old neighbour was run down in the street. My father knew him, said he 'was inoffensive, would have harmed no one'. Troops shot two men dead.

Every Catholic in the west of the city had relatives or friends in those streets or could trace roots back there. Women, pushing prams and children, marched in protest to army lines. I ran to the corner of the street and tagged along behind as they forced their way past confused soldiers who seemed to have no orders for such an eventuality. The curfew ended any hope of civility between locals and the army. Guns were seized, the army claiming this a success, but stories emerged of heavy-handed, downright brutal squaddies. Some accounts were false, many exaggerated, a lot true.

That September, parents were relieved to get us away from the drama of the streets and back to school. Excitedly at first, we exchanged our stories of holidays. The most exotic destinations were a day or two in Dublin or a caravan in Donegal. Things quickly settled, falling into the rote of reading, writing and long multiplication tables.

Jimmy Prentice's class had little of the routine. The most popular teacher in the school, he was outwardly tough about lessons and homework, yet had the human sense to go lightly on youngsters who might have had more worries in their lives. On days when there was shooting, those of us who lived furthest away from the new school or in dangerous places, like close to the barracks, he would pile into the back of his little car, dropping us off at our front doors. Almost by instinct, he finished the run as the first cracks echoed in the streets. At the time, he seemed this big grown man. A black leather jacket set him apart generationally from the rest of the staff. He could not have been aged more than twenty-two. He kicked football with us in the play area out the back of the school or on the fields we shared with the secondary, and he allowed time for painting and singing. He was the first to teach us songs in Irish and Irish songs.

'Show me a man who does not love the land where he was born, who does not look on it with pride no matter how forlorn.'

Back then we did not know what forlorn meant. We had the rest of our lives to find out.

Two army Land Rovers pulled right into the crowded playground on one of those early September days. Both vehicles open, no armour, no covering, just a welded vertical bar to thwart ropes that were being strung neck-high across streets at night.

Four soldiers sat in each jeep, two in front, two sprawled across the back benches; maroon berets, big black and brown rifles, and young smiles. They threw sweets to some of the nearest scrambling for Black Jacks, chews and toffees. Why the soldiers were there at all I do not know. Perhaps they were trying to familiarise themselves with their patch, maybe it was an attempt to improve relations with the community. Soldiers had never been in the playground before. Even so, the mood felt different from when they had first arrived, playing their football with local boys and their brass band's Sunday morning parades. Instinctively I moved to the fringe of the tarmac. Around me, classmates were stooping, furtively, picking up stones, rocks, anything they could throw. There was no pause for politics or reason. It felt natural. I found a stone that fitted snugly in my palm, feeling it, measuring its weight, calculating its flight.

The soldiers waved their goodbyes to the youngsters clambering on the jeeps, shooing them away and revving the throaty engines. It all happened at once. A kid up the front, he could not have been more than six, swung at the side of the first Land Rover with his schoolbag. Everyone else bolted back as though at the sound of a starting pistol. Nothing had been pre-arranged. Something more primitive was at work. All at once, those at the edge threw their missiles in a high arc. You could see your own stone only for a second before it merged into what looked like a murmuration blackening the sky. Those closer bent to pick up stones and as if in one motion lashed them at the jeeps. If there were 200 kids around the soldiers, then almost as many stones and rocks must have been unleashed. Three Paras went down. I saw the blood bright red on one ashen face, spurting just above the temple, making it seem as though his beret was draining colour. The drivers took off circling the playground at speed, kids running everywhere and still skimming stones at them as though back by seaside waves. Four of us shied into a doorway as one of the jeeps sped past a few feet away. It felt like it was going at a hundred miles an hour, like we were in a film, our own action adventure. The bell rang as the vehicles exited the gates. We cheered victory. We strode into class, chests out, hooked by the nose on our first real scent of adrenalin.

Jimmy Prentice looked at us, all mad-eyed, and knew something had changed. He spent the rest of that year attempting to channel the adrenalin in our veins to reinforce us against a world of chaos. No one else would have tried.

No one, except for Micky Barr.

An older family man, with a son already in a class further down the school, he could play the piano. It was an incongruous talent for someone with the frame of a midfielder, who was competitive with other teachers when his class team took to the pitch to play soccer, Gaelic football or hurling.

He prepared us for the 'qually' as we called it, the qualification exam better known as the Eleven Plus. For some of us, two papers sat in the winter of the year would be the most important exams of our lives. We did not know this at the time. Micky Barr did, putting all his energy into ensuring we had at least the chance to take whatever opportunities were going.

Class had its own basic rhythm through the week. On Monday mornings, we entered fresh from the mayhem of the weekend. BBC radio had a schools' programme where, with an accompanying booklet, we sang songs from around the world. We were told that 'My Love's an Arbutus' was the Irish selection. If that did not sound promising, the first time we heard it, a courtly Edwardian love song with nationalistic undertones, we stared at each other's faces, half disbelieving, half deflated. Home radios had been tuned for months to Radio Free Belfast. The station's turntable must have worn thin many vinyls of 'The Men Behind the Wire'. Its catchy and rousing verses were penned, it seemed, in 1971, almost as internment without trial was taking place. It was broadcast around the clock on the short-wave above-the-bar pirate station. The BBC's offering was altogether more pastoral. Still, we rendered 'My Love's an Arbutus' with a patriotic fervour that Alfred Perceval Graves never intended, singing it out as though the crude, wooden-boxed classroom radio was a transmitter as well as a receiver. Afterwards we were calmer and would be put through our paces on the previous weekend's homework, usually a spelling exercise accompanied by the recitation of some mathematic tables. Where Jimmy Prentice showed latitude, Barr treated all with an equally fierce rigour. He had to get us through the exam.

At midday, routine dictated that Barr collect dinner money for the entire school and issue payment tickets for the week ahead. Different colours signified varying levels of the welfare money received by parents. Such was Barr's expertise that the whole process was completed in absolute anonymity with a minimum of fuss. Proceeds counted, we were set work to complete and, small leather bag in hand, off he went to lodge the money in the bank.

The most dangerous half hour in the school week ensued.

Left to our own devices, there was pandemonium. Biro pens, their ends broken by a precise stamp of a heel, were used as peashooters. We had no peas, instead using barley harvested from our mothers' cupboards. Cheeks loaded with barley, a controlled intake and output of breath allowed the tubes to fire just like grown-up guns: single shot through to full automatic. In minutes, the classroom floor was carpeted. Other times an individual might be singled out for some transgression, real or imagined. One lad was pinned firm to the top of desks by seven or eight others while another 'operated' on his ear with the sharp end of a mathematical compass.

One Monday the bell sounded repeatedly and the entire school was evacuated. From our second-floor vantage point, we watched other classes crocodile towards the playing fields to line up for counting. With Micky Barr away making the lodgement, we stayed put.

Johnny Dempsey, a classmate almost continually in trouble, ventured out alone into the hallway. Just then, a teacher called McCabe, who was notionally responsible for us, realised, as he stared back at the school, that we were still in place despite what was an actual real bomb scare. We saw him physically jump, then run back to the building. He arrived on our upper-floor corridor in time to find Dempsey rifling through coat pockets in the hall cloakroom. A chase straight out of a Buster Keaton movie followed. In the middle of the bomb alert we were treated to the spectacle of Dempsey running screaming around the class, screaming louder than the rest of us each time his rump felt the lash of McCabe's flailing leather strap. When order was eventually restored, we left as the other classes tried to re-enter, the scare over. That led to more confusion and fisticuffs as we stormed the door in what became known, for a day or two, as the Bomb Scare Battle.

Ironically, there actually was explosive and other weaponry in the school. No one knew until two men showed up and retrieved gelignite and two handguns from behind a radiator.

The Troubles were just there, part of our normal. It was hardly even a talking point that a couple of lads' fathers were interned. Two of us were put out of our homes and living between family and friends' houses. The school itself was used as a refugee centre in 1971, delaying our restart for a fortnight. That year we were in Mulvenna's class. A kid stood to read his 'what my father does' essay. He proclaimed: 'My father has a machine-gun. He keeps it in the attic. He says it's a Hoover but …' That was as far as he got before a cuff on the ear from Mulvenna. 'Don't be telling those lies about your father; you'll get him in trouble.'

One fella in our class was shot. A bullet put a middle shade up his head. Off for six weeks, when he came back he was a minor celebrity for a full morning until the novelty wore off.

Truth be told, the Troubles caused less terror than 'Fitzy'. Occasionally he snaked into a classroom, bringing with him a chill and his constant companion, the bamboo cane.

The year Mulvenna taught us, Fitzy bounded into our temporary classroom on the side of the playground, breaking through its imaginary separation from the rest of the school.

'Who was playing football on the hill before the lunch bell went?'

Open-eyed I looked around my classmates. We had all been there, every one of us. It was our pitch, just as the P1s and P2s had space in the actual playground and the P7s dominated a portion of the proper football field. Everyone knew we played there, every day, mornings and lunchtime.

'Which of you were there?'

Mulvenna shifted uneasily in his seat.

'Never lie,' my father had always told me. An only child, Enid Blyton had created a world of truthfulness in my head. My hand rose as if borne by the entire Secret Seven. Later, much later, I realised Fitzy was out to thrash the whole class. My owning up threw him. Colour rose in his cheeks making them momentarily less sallow.

'You, you,' it was all exclamation marks. I very much doubt he respected my honesty but rather think he remembered his encounter with my mother.

'Who else? Who else?' he screeched. He was screeching at me. His spit hit my forehead. I was six again, that cane lashing down on my hand. Seanie McKeown, sitting across from me, had not been playing because of a broken arm. 'He wouldn't hit somebody with a plaster cast,' I reasoned. I was right. I pointed at Seanie, who stared back at me, horror all over his face.

'Who else? Who else?' Fitzy was screaming at him now. I had not counted on Seanie cracking as quickly as me: 'Him, him, him, him, him and him.'

Fitzy trailed seven or eight out to the front of the class, Seanie and I were left in our seats as he set about them, the cane whooshing and swishing through their yells of pain. Dempsey was there, of course, and Fitzy pounced on him, shoving him so hard he hit the bar on the emergency door and spun through it, pausing for the merest moment in mid-air before thumping on to the ground five feet below. With that, Fitzsimmons was gone, away back to the main building and his office.

'You shouldn't tell on each other,' Mulvenna said. He spoke to the entire class but looked at me. I felt guilty in the way I would have liked to have gone to confession. 'Bless me Father for I have sinned, I told the truth.'

Funny enough, in a class where everyone blamed everyone else all of the time for everything, such was the common fear of Fitzy that there was no recrimination.

Micky Barr's class was safe. Fitzy never came there or bothered us. Presumably winding down to retirement and having bought a new car, he would sail through the gates at lunchtime and sometimes would not return. One of my uncles saw him on a Sunday afternoon, out in his shirtsleeves, still wearing a tie, washing and waxing his shiny new lime-green Renault. I detected that the uncle, on seeing him, still felt a shudder.

Starting on Monday afternoons, Barr would start putting us through the serious work for the 'qually'. Sums, spelling, reading, sums, spelling, reading, sums, spelling, reading; that would be the catechism for the rest of the week, save maybe on a Thursday or Friday afternoon. We sat in class, numbers one to thirty-six, in order of how we fared in class tests sat at Christmas and Easter. I was towards the top end. Johnny Dempsey was number thirty-one.

Barr and Dempsey had a strained relationship. As poor as Dempsey was at anything academic, he was athletically superb, leading on sports day and in every competition against other classes. He was a loser in tests, a winner on the field. The pressure, though, was on for the tests and Barr drove everyone. Every day Dempsey had a problem; no homework, wrong sums, missed spellings, lost books. Each day Barr would have to resort to the strap. It was administered with a lack of enthusiasm, yet hardly a day passed without Dempsey being brought to the front of the class, the drawer opened and the leather strap wielded. The way Dempsey yelled, timing a jump to minimise the impact on his hand, added to our merriment. Just landing a token stroke became something of a battle of wits between teacher and pupil.

By the summer term, there were other battles.

Soldiers timed their patrols to coincide with our lunch and home times. Our parents and teachers warned us to keep our distance, for the IRA would try to ambush them at the same times. Once, running home to my grandmother's for lunch, I bumped squarely into a man with an Armalite. 'Sorry son.' I was mesmerised by the gun, beautifully sinister and much more futuristic than the longer rifles carried by soldiers.

On an afternoon dander home, a few of us came on three men with a jackhammer. Having spotted an armoured car driving along the estate of new houses, they were trying to place a landmine. We took cover in an entry, watching them closely. Failing to break through fresh-laid concrete, one of the men, clearly frustrated, tossed the bomb into a haversack. Seeing this, we moved further up the entry. They positioned themselves at the bottom. There they contented themselves by blazing away with their big rifle and chirpy little machine gun. Separated by a few paces we had a ring-side view, running only when shots came in uncomfortably close overhead. Adults had been warned to clear the streets and only the soldiers, the IRA and ourselves were present.

Another day, for the first time, a soldier stopped me in the street not far from my grandmother's house. He took my schoolbag, poking his hand inside. At the time, I saw the uniform, this man with a gun going through my belongings, and his fear. He had to be under twenty, scared to be in this alien place with these sullen, silent, resentful natives. All the while his eyes skipped over the streetscape for any twitch of a curtain, glint of metal, any hint of threat.

Of course, we too were a threat. Rioting was fun. To keep us off the streets, in St Paul's Hall of a Saturday afternoon and some summer evenings we watched cowboy films probably first shown to our fathers. For us, every bit as reckless as Crazy Horse, the jeeps, Saracens and Ferret cars were the iron horses invading our plains. Our war dances were atop the gutted skeletons of lorries and vans. Serious riots had petrol and blast bombs. Bigger lads would deploy the occasional ball-bearing-firing catapult. Overwhelmingly, for us, thrown stones and bottles were our arrows of choice. They had no impact whatsoever on the armour, although the sound of rock on metal was compelling, gratifying.

In smaller groups, the sporadic stone was more a symbolic effort. We were vulnerable. Soldiers used air rifles to count coup. Gradually rubber bullets replaced the eye-peeling CS, which forced uncontrollable weeping, coughing and nausea. Old people in the tacky rows really suffered when the gas crept through their homes. It was not the same deterrent for youths who danced through the mist, some kicking the canisters back, perhaps holding vinegar-soaked rags in front of their mouths and noses. We knew the rubber bullets could be lethal and constantly scoured army lines and vehicles for any appearance of the tell-tale thick black barrels.

Still, when a crowd of us happened in the same spot at the same time, power seemed drawn from having others at your shoulder and all around. We were less afraid, keener to prove ourselves, more immortal. 'Bricking the Brits', when they appeared, substituted for lunchtime football.

On a sunny afternoon, a 'Pig' drove up the street just below the school. We knew, with no escape at the top of the street, it would have to return and, whooping with excitement and scrambling for rocks, we ran to the traditional ambush spot. We were all there: Dessie and Marty, Frankie and Paddy. Johnny Dempsey, as always, flew at the head of our column. We reached the corner as we heard the unmistakable engine whine as it slowed. The nearby waste ground provided us with more ammunition. We moved in a shoal, darting from the alleys and from behind walls to launch the first volley. Tiny streets were filled with the sound of rocks on metal and glass breaking on armour. Almost simultaneously, the soldiers slammed shut hatches. Out of cowardice I timed my run fractionally late and as I released my 'halfer' – half brick – a soldier popped his head up to put the back slat on the 'Pig' into position. Direct hit. The face tumbled back into the darkness. I thought nothing. I felt nothing. I was already flinging the next stone.

The engine roared as the 'Pig' pulled away beyond our range. I watched as Dempsey loosed what was probably his fourth or fifth rock, a full brick. It was in the air as the lime green car rounded the corner and, with us suspended in horror, the missile crashed down onto the Renault's exquisitely polished bonnet, somehow missed the windscreen and bounced, audibly, onto and along the equally waxed roof.

All of us saw what happened; the damage, Fitzy's bulging eyes, the terror on Dempsey's face. We scattered in every direction, the shoal now reacting as if a shark had suddenly appeared. We were intent on individual self-preservation, more afraid of Fitzy than any squadron of armoured cars.

Within ten minutes the bell rang and we were sitting panting and sweaty in Micky Barr's second-floor classroom. He started the class as usual, sums. None of us were seeing anything except the dents on Fitzy's car. It was then we heard the door slam and the shouting at McCabe's class at the far end of the corridor. There was more shouting. We knew it was Fitzy. He was on the warpath. Then that door slammed and we heard another flung open, cracking back on its hinges, more from Fitzy. We could not make out what he was yelling. Barr was now distracted by the corridor crescendo and glanced around our class for any clue. His eyes lit on Dempsey, the personification of guilt. All of us who had been there, that is to say all but a few, were looking at Dempsey. Another door slammed, more shouts. We were next. Barr raised his eyebrows as if in interrogation. Dempsey shook his head as if in confirmation, fear etched on his face. The door almost came off the frame.

'Was it any of you? Was it any of you?' Fitzy's face was puce, not dissimilar to the colour of his car.

'Can I help you Mr Fitzsimmons?' Micky Barr was moving out as if to defend us, but Fitzy was having none of it.

He had spied me sitting in the front row and rounded Barr.

'Do you know who did it? Do you know?' Fitzy was above my desk, cane in hand, glaring directly. 'Stand up you.'

Three things went through my head simultaneously: 'never lie son' – my father's words, what had happened the previous year, and the stares of the Secret Seven. I looked around the room, them all looking at me save Dempsey, whose head was in his hands at the far side of the class.

'I don't know what you're talking about, sir,' I replied, evenly, looking at him square in those piercing eyes.

'He's right Mr Fitzsimmons,' said Micky Barr. 'They've all been in here doing extra work for this past half hour.'

Barr towered over him and, in that moment, Fitzy seemed to shrink, showing his frailty. Fight left him. In that moment, he became an old man. Muttering something descriptive, he went to the door. He did not slam it nearly as hard but on the way out caught his cane in the jamb as it dragged behind. It snapped. He kept on going. The door remained a quarter open.

'Close the door for Mr Fitzsimmons, Dempsey,' said Micky Barr. Dempsey rose, relieved to the point of speechlessness, and moved to the door. He hardly had the strength to turn the handle.

'Put that stick in the bin Kelters.'

I walked over to where the half cane lay, broke it in half again and brought it to the bin.

Micky Barr surveyed the class. I thought I saw the trace of a wink at Dempsey and, just as quickly, the lightest of grins toward me.

'Right boys,' he said, 'time for another lesson.'

Begging

In my memory he looks forever like the supporting actor in John Wayne films, the long eccentric man whose only desire was a roof over his head and a rocking chair. He had the same gaunt cheeks, set-back eyes and kindly, innocent smile. He usually arrived late of an afternoon. I would be in from school and there would be a gentle rap on the door. The first time I opened it, he smiled and looked down at me almost apologetically.

'Would Mrs Toner be in?'

I stared at his long tan coat and tan cap. Under the coat was a jacket, shirt and tie in variations of russet. The outfit cast a hue like the skin of a pale onion on his face and hands, giving him every appearance of a singular tan tone.

I knew Clancy. He called at my grandmother's home perhaps once every three or four months. This was the first time I was acting as gatekeeper and I was unsure of myself. My grandmother removed the indecision.

'Clancy, it's yourself, come on in. Sure sit there by the fire.'

Her welcome was warm and comfortable. Clancy took my grandfather's seat. Anywhere between fifty and seventy, I could not have aged him with any accuracy.

'Terrible times, terrible times so they are, Mrs Toner.'

My grandmother was already fetching the crockery from the top shelf in the press. Almost instantly, it seemed, a cup and saucer were on the table and she was pouring tea. As the conversation continued, if it was close to dinner time she immediately served up whatever was on the stove on the best of plates. If it was earlier, something hot and fresh-made was soon on the table.

As my grandmother fussed around the scullery, Clancy sat at the table and regaled us with tales from across the town. There was a mixture of mundane and mayhem. A new wool store had opened in Andersonstown, people were saying it was even cheaper than Delaney's, the shop on the front of the Springfield Road where my grandmother bought her needles, threads and fabric. A woman in the Markets 'is having to raise four childer by herself after her man was shot by the army and she's not getting a penny for him'. There are jobs going in 'some electric factory making stereos' in Dunmurry. A new road has just opened in the east of the city and no one can believe how fast the cars are going. A man in north Belfast was 'giving his chimpanzee to the zoo because it was getting too big'. Nearly two dozen people are living in one house in Ardoyne 'after the young ones were put out of their own houses'.

Those bald lines do him an injustice for he was a natural *seanchaí*, a storyteller peppering his accounts with nuggets of character.

Pages turned on the sequels with his next visit. People were saying the wool from the Andersonstown shop had come from China and was of a different quality. The woman had found a new man. The 'new electric factory' had stopped taking on trainees, a shortcut gets around the new road. The monkey was settling into the zoo, where they were having to wean him off cigarettes. The Housing Executive had suggested some people from Ardoyne move to Craigavon – 'Craigavon, have you ever heard the like, Mrs Toner?'

I noticed that when Clancy told a sad story he exuded genuine sympathy. Every pore was empathetic, his face doleful, his voice resonating low. If it was about something new there was absolute wonder in the way he extended his words, and when it centred on some human triumph, big or small, there was unchecked pleasure and that big toothy smile. The overall effect was hypnotic. More animated than any newsreader, Clancy's stories were raw and real. They meant something to him and for that reason they meant something to the rest of us.

Like my grandmother, I began to welcome Clancy's unannounced visits. Even in winter or on a dreary wet day he did not stay long. Once he had eaten, he took his cup of tea by the fire, usually with a bun or slice of home-made apple cake, tossing in a couple more accounts of the far reaches of the city, districts with names that conjured poetry like Ballyhackamore, Short Strand, New Lodge and Stranmillis. When he finished, he stood up, declaring, 'I'm away now, Mrs Toner, so I am.'

My grandmother would accompany him down the hall to the door, pressing her hand into his. Never once, even after I realised what was going on, did I see her give him the money.

'Ah thanks now, Mrs Toner. That's very good of you all together so it is.'

I wanted to know more about Clancy. Where did he live? Had he a family? How did we know him? Was that his last name? My grandmother told me she did not know, that he had just turned up one day and that it was the only name he had use for, the only name he had ever given. He was a very smart man, she said, who travelled a different way. I asked what she meant; she did not elaborate.

After one visit I determined to follow him, slipping out the door a minute after he left. Cavendish Street was a long street, history in its inception. Built around the turn of the century for the poor coming to work in the mills, it was named after some English lord who had been assassinated in Dublin. The houses, it was said, cost £100 each when new. Now, seventy years later, all the occupants were still paying their weekly rents. Pointing directly at Divis, the first row of maybe more than forty houses stretched a considerable distance down to a dog-leg to the right.

It was a bright May afternoon. I could pick out Clancy's browny-yellow coat against the red brick. Afraid of losing him if he turned onto Oakman Street, I half-skipped with relief when he kept to the main street. He walked purposefully, not quickly, deliberately. Staying in Cavendish Street, I was on familiar ground. I saw the door of one of my friend's homes beyond Gortfin Street, a strange little row where the tarmac ended in a muddy waste ground and the houses petered out. I had been told part of Cavendish Street was built over a river course. I always thought it might have explained the mud that always seemed to be there.

Further along there were what everyone called the 'new houses'. They replaced a cavity gouged out of the terrace by the Luftwaffe. I thought perhaps Clancy would stick to the main street but, with hardly a glance, he crossed, heading up Iris Street towards the Springfield Road.

Forgotten were any warnings about straying across the main road. I was intent on Clancy's destination. Watching him, I saw he greeted each passer-by, saying some hello to men, doffing his cap to women, sometimes patting their small children on the head, all smiling, swapping words about the weather. I was less than fifty yards behind.

About another fifty yards on he turned into Dunmore Street. I was secure. Friends, the Maginns, lived here and my father and I called in on the way home from Mass at Clonard Monastery. Most Monday evenings I covered the same route to go to the boys' confraternity. A Redemptorist would preach from the big wooden pulpit incorporating some story that was intended to be funny. Another priest recited the benediction: 'Blessed be God, blessed be his holy name, blessed be Jesus Christ, true God and true man, blessed be his most Sacred Heart, blessed be his most Precious Blood.' Us quickly repeating each phrase in turn, the words took on the cadence of the multiplication tables we recited in class. Incense was more heady than gas. About 300 of us from all the neighbouring schools would sing in Latin, giving full throat to the opening lyric 'Tantum ergo Sacramentum', before our volume tailed off into ignorance.

I was trying to remember the next line when, suddenly, Clancy stopped and knocked a door. He straightened his tie ever so slightly with his free hand. The door opened and I heard a man speak.

'Ach Clancy. Come on in.'

Pacing up and down, I waited, trying not to appear up to anything in particular. The shadow of a tall factory chimney passing each door and window made the street into a giant sundial. Each time I reached the corner of the street, back at the main road, I would turn and mark it roll away from me one brick at a time towards Clonard.

Some twenty minutes later Clancy emerged as quickly as he had entered.

'Look after yerself, Mr Crane, now. Let those wee gran-childer take care of you a bit.'

The now identified man waved his goodbye. Clancy did not notice me. It must have been after five o'clock. A few of the Mackies men were in the street and others were returning home from the opposite direction. I needed to be back at my grandmother's for dinner. She might be anxious. Clancy turned into Clonard Street. I was off, close behind down the hill. Again, this was familiar terrain. Linden Street, where I was born, was just over the way. From as early as I could remember I knew so many there. Also born there, my father could name the family behind each door.

Clancy knocked at another door and was admitted. I was too far back to grab any conversation. I waited again, this time studying a pile of rubble further along the street. IRA men had been making a bomb and it exploded, taking down the house they were in and the others on either side. I had heard the crumple of the detonation, and a short time later word came up the road that all the IRA who had been in the house were killed. I wondered if this was what Cavendish Street looked like after the German bomb.

Clancy came out and headed off into a side street. Hesitant in mind, my feet kept following. It struck me he had quickened his step. Sure enough, I was almost trotting to keep pace. He soon took another sharp right, then left, and we were back on the main Falls Road passing the library. The head librarian was a friend of my father's, so I could take out as many books as I wanted. The Clonard Picture House was across the road. I had never known it open, but my father always spoke of it wistfully, so even with litter piled behind the railings across its doors it felt somehow safe and familiar. Clancy and I continued, tied by an invisible connection. Buses were passing, packed with office workers from the city. Briefly it crossed my mind that my mother might see me.

At the next street corner, he walked directly through the door of Charlie Daly's pub. Again, I walked up and down, this time thinking about my grandmother's dinner. I turned for home and was almost back at the library when I looked over my shoulder. The tan coat and cap emerged from the bar. I pursued.

Clancy was walking faster now. I was at a full run, both of us staying to the main road. This, I knew, was stretching boundaries. Relatives lived below St Peter's. Its spires once dominated the district but now it was over-shadowed by Divis Tower. Two hundred feet tall with a sandbagged army position on top, it sat amid a dozen concrete tiered blocks that replaced little streets of the district. When it was built people were promised little palaces in the air. Nothing could have been further from the truth. Redevelopment untied generations of neigh-bours. Fire had already devastated the left side of the road where the big mills dominated just a few years previously. Hoardings concealed the removal of debris. The mill at Conway Street and the Falls Road baths were the only big buildings standing. Clancy hurried on, taking me beyond my routine horizon.

We were almost at the foot of Divis Tower when he disappeared into a big house. This time there was no knock on the door. I sensed he would not be reappearing. I examined the house. Four storeys high, it looked tatty, uncared for, unkept. Paint on the door and window frames was flaking. The windows themselves had a variety of curtains, all of them drawn, all of them grey. Most noticeable, in the downstairs window there was a statue of the Child of Prague, too big for the window, too small for a church.

I dodged the traffic and crossed the road. I stopped just some little ways up, outside a school. I stared at a bunch of flowers tied to its railings and at the bottom of its steps where there was a makeshift wooden cross.

'They shot our teacher there.'

A lad about my age was watching me.

'When did that happen?'

'Not too long ago, we all got the day off to go to the funeral.'

He was friendly. I ventured another question.

'What's that place over there?' I indicated towards the house where Clancy had gone.

'The one with the blue door?'

'Yeah.'

'That's the tramps' house. You don't want to go near that. They're like bogeymen so they are.'

This did not square with Clancy. My face betrayed no emotion. He had a watch.

'Do you have the time?'

'You ask a lot of questions, so you do. It's twenty to six.'

'Thanks.'

I was already trotting away. I remained on the Falls, not crossing until near Clonard Street, past Linden Street, Waterford Street, McQuillan Street; past all the shops I knew, the Dunville Medical Hall, the Post Office, the home bakery and, on the corner, Lena's sweet shop. I was panting and sweating as I reached the pietà at the back of St Paul's, knowing I was almost home. I thought of my grandmother worrying. I reached the house just as my uncle, returning from work, got out of his car. We walked in together, confusing my grandmother just long enough for me to escape scolding. She was always relieved when anyone came home. Dinner was put on the table, steam rising from the potatoes, cabbage and bacon. The running had given me an appetite and my grandmother looked on approvingly as I set about it with enthusiasm.

'Nana?

'Yes son?'

'Is Clancy a tramp?'

Silence.

My grandmother put down her fork and stared at me.

'Seamus,' she said. Her tone told me I had erred. 'Have you ever heard Clancy say anything bad about anybody?'

I thought for a moment about Clancy's stories. They were sad, informative and funny but, no, I had never heard him speak ill of any individual. He was not complimentary about soldiers. Who was? Other than that, his accounts always showed people in their best light, overcoming challenges, being kind.

'No,' I murmured.

'No. So why would you say that about Clancy? We are lucky to have him as our friend aren't we?'

I felt my lower lip quiver. 'Yes, we are.'

'Has he ever said anything bad?'

'No.'

I did not know how, yet it was clear I had disappointed my grandmother.

'Clancy,' she said, 'is one of those people who makes things better for the rest of us and there's not too many of them about these times.'

'There is not.' My grandfather chipped in his agreement.

'You'll not say that again, will you?'

My grandmother fixed me with her sternest gaze, not so much looking at me as into me.

'No. Sorry.'

She smiled a faint smile at me. 'It's all right son. Do you want a bit of apple cake?

I nodded to get her to go away, so she would not see welling tears.

That night, as he knelt to say his rosary, my grandfather told me to say a prayer for Clancy. I had never prayed with such fervour.

True to his fashion, Clancy arrived at the door about four months later, on a grey autumn afternoon. At first his presence stirred my guilt. I could not look him in the eye until his stories set me at ease. The zoo had given the chimpanzee back to the man because they felt it was homesick. It was back on ten Benson and Hedges a day. My grandmother and I laughed hard.

Fed and watered, Clancy rose to leave and my grandmother grasped his hand.

'Ach thanks, Mrs Toner. You're one of the best so you are.'

Off he went, the same coat billowing behind him against a chilled breeze and threat of rain. We watched him go. I did not think of following.

'Clancy's a nice man isn't he, Nana?'

'He is son. He is a very nice man.'

My grandmother moved four years later. As long as the family lived in Cavendish Street, Clancy's periodic visits had continued. He and a tradition of community telegraph and community care were lost to the confusion of redevelopment, upheaval and uncertainty. Sometimes yet, I fancy I see him in those changed places through a distinctive gait or particular colour of long coat. He said he would be sure to visit at the new family home. It was a few miles away at Finaghy. He never did. We never saw Clancy again.

Duck

A class trip was something spoken of as though Christmas was coming in May. From before Easter, money was collected by our teacher. I do not remember how much it cost per head, perhaps three or four pounds. It was after decimalisation, but a pound still counted for something. This was big money, so the collection was going on for weeks, anxiety building over whether we would all be able to go.

'Have you paid yet?'

'No, have you?'

The questions and answers littered every conversation.

The threat of being kicked off the trip hung over our every misdemeanour, so we were subdued at least in class and when teachers were around. A student teacher spent some of the time teaching us about Cú Chulainn. Here was a hero we could identify with, bold, brave and reckless. The student might have been his image, in a mirror, in reverse. Uncharacteristically for us, for we scented fear, we took no advantage of his obvious naivety even when our teacher, Micky Barr, was not watching. A class trip was not to be risked.

We had been on our first day out the previous year. About half of us had already been brought to Belfast's zoo, Bellevue we called it back then, even before the class trip. It was a wet day. The hillside collection of semi-domesticated elephants, giraffes and kangaroos was miserable, shrouded in mizzle. We packed close together in front of the lion enclosure.

'There's no lion in there so there's not,' shouted one of the class.

In fact, the cage's sole occupant, wisely, remained under the coverage of foliage at the back where, barely visible, it refused to respond to our roars.

We ventured into the monkey house, its pungency making our eyes water. There came the highlight of the day. Some classmates were taunting a huge silverback gorilla. Infuriated, it flung some of its faeces at us. We charged away, tripping over each other, laughing at those we claimed had been successfully targeted.

'You've got monkey shite on you.'

'No I haven't.'

'Yes you do.'

'You are monkey shite.'

Other visitors, from more well-heeled areas, viewed us with disdain. 'They should be on the other side of the bars,' I heard a woman say as she dragged her child away.

We had not gone far that day and there was little to marvel at through the rain.

Expectation for the new class trip was fuelled by one of the class who had been there on holiday. Dessie Burns painted a picture of a land somewhere between Glocca Morra and Shangri-La.

'There's big aeroplanes so there is,' he told us, 'and they fly way up in the sky so they do.'

Each week the stories of what we would find inflated; dodgems, a swimming pool, boats, rides, ice cream, snooker tables, toy stores and arcades. And, once you got through the gates, Dessie said, it was all free.

We were going to Butlin's Mosney.

The day arrived. The buses arrived. We spat on board like fizzy drink shaken from a bottle, scrambling to get to the back seats beyond the view of the teachers at the front. Well before safety regulations, in some cases three or four of us piled into two seats. In the same way three classes were crammed onto two buses, more than a hundred of us accompanied by a trio of teachers and as many students. My berth was midway.

The talk was, not everyone had paid their full amount, although Micky Barr saw to it that every boy in his class got on the bus. Tickets might have been subsidised from school funds. More likely, the money came from his pocket.

Mosney was about five miles beyond Drogheda, a journey for us of about 80 miles. The first problem emerged about 20 minutes after we left the school. We had been told to bring packed lunches. For some these consisted of chocolate of every variety, cans of fizzy orange and unlimited quantities of crisps. As we twisted along country roads, there was an unmistakable 'whooooahhh' from up the front as one of our class, Paddy McIlwaine, retched into a carrier bag that had contained his lunch.

'Wow.'

'Ah shite.'

'Move, move.'

Those around him scattered as if he had unpinned a live grenade. They fled into neighbouring rows ignoring the occupants' protests. Paddy was left to himself. The student teacher reached back to open a latched sliding pane above one of the big windows. Air rushed down the bus, along with the smell.

Seeing the student open the window, some of those at the back of the bus did the same with a window there. Marty Breen went a step further, clambering on a seat to yell out the window. It was not so much that he actually said anything, just the fact that he made some sort of roar to startle pedestrians. Each time he saw someone walking, he would let out a high-pitched 'yeeeeee-oow'.

The more this amused the rest of us, the more audacious he became. He shouted 'fatso' at a man, and 'millies' at two girls. The Belfast jibe might have been lost on them, but we laughed anyway at the shock on their faces.

What happened next, as somehow unlikely as it was predictable, I watched as though in slow motion. Looking out the front window of the bus, I saw a crowd waiting at a stop. A couple moved forward thinking we were the scheduled service. A lot of us saw them. Marty Breen saw them and turned his head sideways to get as much out of the open window as possible. Up front, Paddy McIlwaine was not a troublemaker, not usually the centre of devilment, but others around him were hissing, 'Go on, go on.' To be fair, he must have wanted to get rid of the bag of boke. As we sped almost level with the bus stop, he neatly threw it out the window. His only misjudgement was the effect speed would have on trajectory. Instead of showering the bystanders, the bag slewed along the side of the bus, catching Marty Breen as he stretched for a high note. Too late someone shouted, 'Duck!' The bag hit him full in the face in mid gulder – 'Yeeee-argh, argh, aww, shite, shite.' He was drenched in vomit, his face, his neck, his hair, his pullover, the collar of the shirt he was wearing. He was simultaneously attempting to splutter and not breathe. Yells came from everywhere around him.

'Get away, get away.'

'Spew face, look at spew face.'

The student teacher came down the bus. He saw the state of Marty and thought he had been sick. You could see the student almost gag himself at the overpowering smell.

'Wooooargh.'

There was the sound of liquid splattering onto plastic. Someone else had puked into another bag. We were cheering, jeering, shouting. Anarchy threatened.

'Quiet. Quiet all of you.'

Micky Barr had come halfway back, his voice raised, close to where I was sitting. 'If youse keep this up, the bus will turn around and you'll all go home.'

Silence. For the first time that day, silence. A wet towel appeared from somewhere. Marty was told to clean himself up.

Micky Barr warned us. 'If there's one more can opened or I hear one more crunch on a crisp between here and Mosney, I'll get the driver to turn back. One more. Do you hear me?'

No one spoke. Lunches, or what was left of them, were stored in overhead racks. Micky Barr, we knew, was not a man of empty threat.

There was little else by way of event, except when we reached the border. Soldiers stationed in a sandbagged emplacement somewhere beyond Newry made a token effort of stopping traffic so that the buses, cars and lorries formed a long queue. We belted out a song. None of the teachers attempted to stop us. We saw the student join in on the refrain: 'Armoured cars and tanks and guns, came to take away our sons'. I had the impression the driver wished someone would take us away. I glimpsed his face in his mirror; it was a look of antipathy. I found this difficult to understand, for everyone where I came from loved 'The Men Behind the Wire'. Exhausting it, we launched into 'The Merry Ploughboy', chanting out the phrase 'to the echo of a Thompson gun'. We had all heard that echo, we could relate to the words.

Micky Barr stood up.

'We have just crossed the border,' he announced and there was a big cheer.

The student teacher was not to be outdone. 'That's the Gap of the North boys – remember, from the stories about Cú Chulainn, the Celtic myths?' He did not get a cheer. Instead, we grunted feigned interest, for he had joined us in the singing and we wanted to reciprocate.

The most obvious indication we were in the Free State were the bilingual signs, Dún Dealgan, Droichead Átha and of course Baile Átha Cliath. The Irish for Dundalk, Drogheda and Dublin respectively was more mysterious and strange on our tongues, mostly because of our twangy Belfast mispronunciations. I learned my Irish at beginners' classes in the Chluain Árd hall in Hawthorn Street, a cold, Spartan building where I demonstrated no facility whatsoever for grasping the language. Despite my ignorance, I loved the sounds, relishing even more the discovery of their meanings.

We passed a sign for the Cooley Peninsula. My father had spent holidays there and, long before the student teacher, he had told me how only the teenage Cú Chulainn had defended Ulster's honour after Queen Medb sent her Connacht men to steal Donn Cúailnge, the great brown bull of Cooley.

The one place on the way to Dublin that always struck me was Castlebellingham, in the townland of Gernons-town, the only village where the Anglicised version, named after some lieutenant of Cromwell, sounded more melodious than the Irish, Baile an Ghearlánaigh.

The road blurred past. We reached Drogheda, rolled down the hill and booed crossing the Boyne, the site of the 1690 battle, a permanent reminder for the defeated. Soon we arrived at the entrance to Butlin's, all standing up with excitement, eager to indulge in its delights.

'Quiet. All of you, quiet.' Micky Barr was standing again. 'Sit down. Sit down while I see if they'll let us in.' We peered intently as he got off and presented the paperwork. Back on the bus, he shouted a few ground rules as we pulled through the gates. We had to be back at the bus by four o'clock and were not to get into any trouble. There might have been more. That was all I heard.

For weeks, my friends and I had planned meticulously where we would go first. When the doors of the bus opened, it uncorked us in a headlong rush. We ran every which way, yelling and squealing to announce our arrival. Whatever I was looking for, I could not find. There were a couple of shops, a sign towards a boating lake, a big open recreation room where some of our lads had already grabbed the few available snooker cues and table-tennis bats. The snooker tables were full-sized, far too big for us, and my classmates were already seeing how hard they could bounce the ball from the far rail.

'Stop that,' shouted Micky Barr. 'If I see that again you are back on the bus.'

The lads had to leave the tables to our teachers. I wondered if King James had felt the same when King Billy chased him from the field.

We darted from place to place, seeing everything inside perhaps 20 minutes. There were accommodation blocks. They were curtained, as were a row of chalets. There was, I think, a roller-skating rink. None of us had skates. There was a swimming pool. None of us had trunks. A local school from Drogheda was there as well and we narrowly made it ahead of them to an empty roundabout of little planes that raised on extended arms about ten feet in the air to circle slowly before descending again.

'Hey Dessie, when were you here?'

Dessie Burns was in one of the planes.

'About five years ago,' he shouted back.

We looked around, the realisation dawning this would be a great place if, that was, you were five.

We amused ourselves by throwing sweets from plane to plane and mimicking machine-gun noises. Paddy McIlwaine puked over the side. No one was below.

When we got off, the pace slowed. The roundabout was one of a few medium-sized fairground rides. Most were tame. We tried to go on the dodgem cars.

'Sure isn't the genny broke now boys,' said a man with a sing-songy southern brogue. 'Have yees tried the aeroplane ride?'

We moved off to eat what was left of our lunches, sitting on benches near a fountain. Others, like army ants, were running backwards and forwards.

'Where are yis going?' asked one of my friends.

'There's a big toy shop down there,' we were told.

We dumped our lunch bags and headed off in hope. It was a reasonably sized shop. It sold toys and sweets. I went inside to find it packed by my schoolmates and youngsters, boys and girls about the same age, from the Drogheda school.

'Look at that, look at that.'

Some of the lads were pointing at alarmingly realistic toy pistols, metal and sleek, James Bond-style, complete with a plastic silencer. There were squabbles as the guns became scarce, classmate after classmate taking them from the shelves. The Drogheda class seemed confused by our fascination. One decided he too wanted a James Bond gun. It started as a tug-of-war.

'It's moine, now, I saw it first,' said the lad from Drogheda.

Two of my class mocked his accent. 'It's moine, it's moine,' they shouted in his face.

'You're nordy troublemakers,' yelled back one of the Drogheda kids.

We did not know what 'nordy' meant. Back home, I had heard a lot worse but knew this was intended and accepted as an insult. One of my class punched him square in the nose. He squealed, and squealed again when he was kicked. Mayhem followed.

A couple of shop assistants, well out of their depth, ran from behind their counters trying to separate the melee. Some of my classmates seized the opportunity, along with all manner of goods, which they secreted in their coats and bags before running from the shop.

A man in a suit appeared, positioning himself by the door.

'Quiet. Stop or I'll call the gardaí.'

His shouts, like those of Micky Barr, had authority above the clamour. We knew the gardaí were the Free State police. Order was restored.

The man stopped one of my classmates leaving.

'What's that you have there?'

'What?' snapped back my classmate.

'That there,' said the man snatching a large toy box out from under my classmate's pullover.

'I bought that, I bought that.' He remonstrated loudly as though volume alone would make his case.

'Oh, did you now?' said the man. 'I suppose you'll be having the receipt then?'

My classmate made a show of searching for an elusive non-existent piece of paper.

'Do you want me to call the gardaí now? Is that what you'll be wanting then, to be put in jail?'

'Go ahead,' said my classmate, but we could tell the confidence had gone. We watched as he was forced resentfully to return the box to its shelf.

'And if you come back the guards will take you away,' said the man shoving him out the door.

We were all frisked leaving. I noticed the Drogheda school was not subjected to the same scrutiny.

Once outside, there was nothing much to do, nothing much to engage eleven-year-olds who could have picked a riot with a squad of soldiers for fun on almost any given lunchtime. Butlin's was more geared to cater for young families than school trips in general or us in particular. It was the first holiday camp the company had opened beyond its traditional base, and to placate the Catholic hierarchy, fearful of creeping English secularism, it apparently agreed to place a church and priest on site. We did not see the church or the priest as we wandered aimlessly. It was probably just as well.

At one point, for want of anything better, we rapped doors along the chalet row and ran off before people answered. It was our game, thunder and lightning; knock the door like thunder and run like lightning. We had another spin on the planes, boring.

A small group of us went back towards the boating lake. Looking harassed, a man there was putting youngsters into rowing boats, four at a time.

'Take it easy now, take it easy or you'll end up in the lake now.'

Two lads from the Drogheda school had the misfortune to be put alongside two of my classmates who commandeered the oars. Out on the water others of my class were already trying to get their boats up to ramming speed.

'No standing,' shouted the man. 'You can't be standing or you'll be falling in.'

Kids from Drogheda were squealing from excitement and genuine fear. The man shouted again. The lake was not that big. My classmates feigned deafness. Gradually, things on the water settled, due principally to fatigue rather than any law of the High Seas. It seemed there was a truce of sorts between the mixed crew. Our lads concentrated on rowing. The Drogheda lads were throwing bits of bread to a few mallards that had ventured out from the big bush or small island in the lake.

'Here duckie, duckies.' I could hear one of the Drogheda crew draw a few drakes to feed.

Observing from the shore it was another slow-motion moment. I could see the intent in our lad's mind as he lifted the oar from its rowlock. The lake was still, even as he brought the oar down. It is perhaps some consolation to believe the duck felt nothing; one moment pecking a piece of watery bread, the next, not. A huge splash made by the flat of the oar, a puff of feathers above the surface, the panicked quacks of the other ducks flapping off across the surface, these were the only evidence.

Following the briefest pause, as what had happened sunk in and the duck sank under, there was the outcry; kids from Drogheda, including those who had given the bread, screaming in horror, the boatman yelling for them to 'Come in, come in.'

A mother who had been wheeling a pram shouted: 'Yees are murderers so yees are, nothing but murderers, that poor wee duck.'

I saw that several of our school on the lake and dotted around the shoreline path were laughing and whooping. Myself and the couple of friends who were with me decided to move on when we saw the man in the suit striding towards the boatman's hut.

It was a quarter to four. We went back to the car park. The Drogheda school's bus was parked close-by, too close. Emotions were still running high after the duck. They were yelling at us. 'Nordies, nordies, yees fucked the duck.'

In spite of our wildness, we did not curse, so this was a serious offence, a challenge. We became Cú Chulainns, Hounds of Ulster. There was a boarding party. I may have been part of it. Some kids on the other bus may have been punched. A window may have cracked.

The other school's teacher turned up. Irate, he lined seven or eight of us against the side of the bus and proceeded to shout, calling us 'savages'.

'Yees are nothing but savages,' he yelled. 'That's what ye are. Is it any wonder Belfast is in the state it's in? I'll get the guards, I will. Which of you broke that window?'

We stared at the ground. It might have been me. I was not sure. He went on.

'Do ye not know how to behave when yer up with decent, civilised people?'

Just at that, our teachers showed up. They had to have heard that final phrase, perhaps the whole tirade, he was so loud. Ignoring protestations from the Drogheda teacher, Micky Barr ordered us back on our own bus. There, noses pressed against the windows, we watched developments. We had heard Micky Barr shout, but never like this. This was new, and for once it was not aimed at us. There might have been cursing. 'You should be bloody well ashamed of yourself so you should. Do you know what these lads have been through?' I thought he was perhaps referring to Paddy McIlwaine and the bag. His cheeks were red, his finger was jabbing into the other man's chest and then, to our surprise, he shoved him, sending him sprockling backwards onto the ground.

'Look at yer man, look at yer man,' shouted my classmates gleefully. 'He's up again, he's up. Look out Mr Barr.'

The student teacher separated them, dragging Micky Barr back to our bus. He sat breathing heavily at the front. 'Well done sir,' said one of our class. Others cheered.

'Yer teacher fights worse than Queen Mebh,' yelled Marty Breen out the window at the other bus. We roared. We saw the student and even Micky Barr laugh as we rode out of the gates of Butlin's.

We stopped briefly in Drogheda for the educational component to the day. We trooped into a church there and paraded in front of Blessed Oliver Plunkett's head, behind glass, inside a gold casket. I looked at it in the same way I had watched the duck; part intrigued, part repulsed. The explanation muttered went along the lines of 'the Brits did it'. We exchanged knowing looks, more subdued when we got back on the bus. It took the sight of soldiers at the border again to rouse us back into another refrain: 'And every man will stand behind the men behind the wire'.

The rest of the trip was quiet, spent mostly showing purchases and flashing toys obtained from the shop. Some were bought, some were plunder. We whispered about the fight with the other school and between the teachers. The popular version now was that Micky Barr had clocked the other teacher, knocking him out cold. We exaggerated too how much we had enjoyed the holiday camp. No one was sick, not even Paddy McIlwaine. Some parents were waiting at the school gates. We made our way home.

The following week the duck came home to roost.

There was the letter from the management of Butlin's. Micky Barr read parts of it. The gist was that as a school we would not be welcome back. Signed by the manager, a line stated that 'the shop on the site had never had so much taken without payment in a single day'. There was also a pointed reference to what was described as 'an incident on the lake which left children from another school shocked'.

Then, there was the complaint from the bus company. Micky Barr did not read it, telling us briefly that their driver had felt intimidated by our behaviour. Finally, the trilogy was completed with a letter from the principal of the Drogheda school. It, Micky Barr said, made a number of unproven claims about us and him and an allegedly broken bus window. The principal of our school, he told us, was furious. It had been decreed that, for the remainder of the year, we were to be barred from playing games, having any paints or art material in class and singing. These were the only activities we enjoyed, the only time we could break away from the sums and spellings. There were groans. Micky Barr's stare stilled us, even the student teacher.

'Well lads,' he said. 'Some of what you did down there was wrong, but I know that you are getting blamed for a lot of it in the wrong too. That's the way it is sometimes in these times.'

We blinked, uncertain if we were being chastised or praised.

He went on: 'Now you can't do any art, but nobody said you can't do drawings, did they?' There was a collective sing-songed, 'No, Mr Barr.' He told us we were to spend the next hour drawing Cú Chulainn and his deeds.

The class cheered. Even the student teacher clapped. Micky Barr smiled.

'You are Belfast boys, not savages. You know what boys?' We were straining for his words now. 'In a lot of years' time, when you are old men, you will remember this. Congratulations, you have created your own myth, your own Ulster Cycle, your own Great Cattle Raid of Cooley.'

Bin-lid

The shooting that night was untempered. Acoustics in the terraces funnelled unfaithful reports, making it difficult to estimate distance, target and firing points. That night there was no question it started far away. The adults reckoned Andersonstown. It was actually just beyond that, in Lenadoon. For several days, it had been quiet. There was some sort of a ceasefire and all the excited talk was of some sort of talks with the British. That night it was obvious any ceasefire was over. Gunfire rippled towards us like a squall rolling down from the mountain.

Suddenly the shooting was unmistakably nearby. As ever, the target would be the barracks. Sometimes there was the zip of the bullets. Occasionally, spent rounds would rattle from the slates into the gutters.

Some years earlier, when the shooting had first started, my grandfather had draped heavy blankets over the windows. This was done in the twenties, he told us, the theory being that the fabric would pull down bullet speed and maybe even act as a stopper. If the tactic had ever worked, back then even my grandfather, despite his gift of authority in his thran country ways, soon realised it was no match for high-velocity rounds and machine guns. So, when gunfire perforated the night there would be no debate and we would take to the floor.

The shooting intensified as dusk turned to darkness. Occasionally there was a glimpse of luminous, hot metal tracer fire. Apart from the gunfire, which would become almost a background bass beat, every other noise seemed to be exaggerated and take on increased significance. There would be no footsteps in the street but perhaps the bark of a dog, distant siren or whine as the driver of an armoured car changed gears to accelerate.

On this particular night, we heard something unheard in a while.

Tat rat, tat rat, rat tat.

It was the unmistakable drumbeat of a bin-lid banged with force, then scraping as it was lifted off concrete. Bin-lids and sometimes whistles were the improvised alarm of choice to warn of the presence of army patrols. Cheap and readily available, they would sound out a street to street, district to district alarm. Despite my grandmother urging him to stay put, my uncle ventured into the parlour. He returned declaring that he could see no sign of soldiers in either direction along the street.

Tat rat, tat rat, rat tat.

It sounded out again. It was more unnerving than the shooting which, though sporadic in its geography, was oddly consistent.

'Maybe I should go out to help.'

My uncle was sympathetic to the lone bin-lid player.

'Catch yourself on,' said my grandmother with uncommon sharpness.

'You didn't see any soldiers,' said my grandfather, torn between community spirit and the steely stare of his wife.

Tat rat, tat rat, rat tat.

There it was again, the statement, the very embodiment of individual resistance.

'They might be in the entry or in the convent grounds.'

There was silence, everyone thinking about my uncle's words.

'Bam. Bam, bam, bam.' A rifle blatter, close by.

A voice cut through the static on the radio. 'Shots fired at Bravo One. Shots fired at Bravo One. No one – repeat no one – injured.' Knowing that the barracks had indeed been the target, all seemed happy to have confirmation of what had happened.

Tuning the transistor to police and army frequencies was part of the ritual of these nights. My grandfather and uncle would take turns, sometimes arguing as they wheeled the knob in and out of channels, each competing for the triumph of hearing an illicit voice.

Of course, local accents would be outnumbered by the English, Welsh or Scots depending on the regiment. We laughed as soldiers tried to pronounce the names of familiar streets. 'Shots near Am-come-rye Street'. Amusement came with the realisation this was Amcomri Street. A lot of streets in Belfast commemorate British military engagements in the Empire's far-off outposts. Amcomri Street, close to my route to school, was unusual in that it was actually built with funds sent by the 'American Committee for the Relief of Ireland'.

On another night, making one of the most dangerous streets in the district sound like a Parisian boulevard, a soldier announced: 'Car stopped at Lee-son Street.' We held ourselves, laughing.

Friends of my grandparents lived in Leeson Street; the Donnelly sisters were three maiden aunts well into their retirement. Frances had worked as a bookkeeper in a big department store in the town. Donna spent years behind the counter of a corner shop, and Teresa had always stayed at home. They enthralled us one night with their story of the Leeson Street trumpet. Passed from house to house, it was meant to be used if any army patrol appeared. Each family, holding the instrument by turn, was expected to keep look-out all night and sound reveille, so to speak, if necessary.

On the evening the Donnellys had the trumpet, they stayed awake making endless cups of tea. Just before dawn, its dented brass glinting reassuringly from the kitchen table, they lapsed into a gentle slumber only disturbed when one woke up to the shadow of a soldier standing at their front window. The sisters panicked, grabbed the trumpet, tiptoed to the scullery and ran to the backyard. There, they were so unpractised, so afraid, their mouths so dry, that they were unable to raise a single note. Oblivious, the army patrol moved on, and the residents of Leeson Street were also none the wiser.

On this night, however, Leeson Street was quiet. My grandmother's street was not.

Tat rat, tat rat, rat tat. The bin-lid again.

It was impossible to sleep.

'I need to go out.' Guilt was overcoming my uncle.

'What good will that do?' My grandfather was un-commonly curt.

'Sit where you are.' My grandmother was typically direct.

Tat rat, tat rat, rat tat.

It was louder than the shooting, which now rippled in the distance again, maybe Lenadoon, maybe Ardoyne, maybe Ballymurphy.

Lying on the floor was uncomfortable at the best of times. These were the not the best of times. The first night we had to take to the floor was in 1969, when the big mills that lined the Falls were burned. As my grandfather dragged me out of bed, I could see the weird glow to the sky, a fiery Belfast aurora that cast a blush on the walls of the room. Lying on the cold, uneven lino, the hearth forming a pillow, I looked up through the back window and saw sparks wave on the breeze. The adults, whispering for no apparent reason, speculated about what might be happening. No one knew for certain.

In subsequent days, I stared in wonderment at the piles of smouldering rubble. How could these impenetrable, towering red-brick edifices have been razed in a single night? It was said the IRA set them on fire to prevent snipers from taking their pot-shots into the district. In truth, no one seemed to be sad. The mill owners' wealth had too often been built on the misery of the poor to extract much sympathy. Mounds of still-warm debris pulled us like magnets and the practical consequence was that most of my class had to go to the doctor because of the skin itching caused by the dust. We were each prescribed big brown bottles of an unknown liquid, painted morning and night onto our arms and legs to sooth the prickling.

Tat rat, tat rat, rat tat.

It was unrelenting.

My grandmother looked uneasily at my uncle.

'What time is it?'

'About half three.'

I drifted off into a neck-creaking sleep. Dawn stopped the shooting. My grandfather or uncle carried me to my bed, where I woke up to the smell of bacon and eggs and the hum of a milk float clinking along the street.

I dressed and went downstairs. I have a notion there was no school that day because it all happened during the July holidays. My uncle and grandfather were off work. My grandmother gave me breakfast.

'That was terrible last night. You missed the worst of it,' said my grandmother, looking at me.

'The shooting?'

'No, that bloody bin-lid.' I'd never heard my grandfather come close to cursing, so this was a surprise.

The eyes of the adults were strained. I doubt they had more than an hour's sleep.

'I should have gone out.' My uncle was still full of self-reproach.

There was a knock at the door. Everyone started. Mrs Smith, the neighbour my grandmother was closest to, was halfway up the hall. In those days, doors always remained ajar.

'Mrs Smith, will you take a wee cup of tea?'

'Just a wee drop in my hand Mrs Toner. God, wasn't that awful?'

'The bin-lid?'

'Aye. They're going to have to do something about him.'

'Who?' My grandfather was intrigued.

'It was Sean,' said Mrs Smith. The Hanrattys lived midway between my grandmother's house and Smith's. Deprived of oxygen at birth, Sean Hanratty had never been to mainstream school but wandered the streets, visiting family friends and relatives in amicable routine. Back then, they called him 'slow'. There was plenty of politics but no political correctness.

'Sure, the lad's not right. I didn't get a wink.'

Mrs Smith, like my grandparents and uncle, was more disturbed by losing sleep than the shooting and it made her more forthright.

'Who else would have been rapping a bin-lid in the middle of all that shooting? It's not as if the army were out of the barracks. Sure, anybody that would do that is a bin-lid himself.'

I saw the colour raise in my uncle's cheeks. He looked guilty again now. Neither of my grandparents dared look in his direction.

Fridays

I stood at the street corner and heard another bomb. It was in the distance, the familiar mix of roar, rumble and crumple, like someone stamping down on a cardboard box. Close at hand, presumably near the bottom gate to the hospital, as well as from the distance, I heard the sirens of ambulances mixed with those of fire brigades and police cars. It was a summer afternoon. I was off school. I moved closer to the Falls and Grosvenor junction. From its slight elevation, I saw at least half a dozen plumes of smoke from the city. Some were steam-chimney grey, others violent billowing black from amid and between the white concrete and red-brick buildings. My parents and grandmother were all in the city. I did not know if I would see them again, if they would survive. There was another explosion somewhere to the south, the sound funnelled along the Bog Meadows. I was terrified.

It was Bloody Friday.

Orange's Civil Service Academy was sited in Chapel Lane next to the oldest Catholic church in the city. In spite of its name and its location, or perhaps because of these, it was non-denominational. Run by a couple of brothers and their sister, such was its reputation that pupils came from all over Belfast and beyond.

'I wanted to be really good at what I did, that's why I went there,' my mother once told me.

Having been raised in a family where money was tight,

she had a solid work ethic. At Orange's she got on well with others from the same circumstances and developed an abiding disdain for journalists sent by their papers to notionally improve their typing and note taking.

'All they were good at was going out to pubs,' she said. 'It was all right for them, they already had their jobs.'

My mother, the younger sister, believed education was key to self-improvement. She begged until her parents paid the fees for her to attend what was essentially a small, private secretarial school. At Orange's she was treated and trained as one about to enter a civil service job, no school uniforms, smart office-like clothes. She liked the staff.

'They were strict, but they pushed you and you learned to do your work right.'

She had an aptitude for Pitman shorthand and touch-typing, practising over and over until she was word perfect and as fast as could be.

As much as she enjoyed picking up the skills, she lived for the end of the week. On Fridays at lunchtime, the academy's pupils could go to a religion class appropriate to their faith or could go home early. In the couple of years she attended, my mother would leave and rush to 'the GNR'. The Great Northern Railway station in Great Victoria Street was her track to freedom. She would run to board a train to Portadown. There she changed for Omagh. Pottering through river valleys and hillside cuttings, past Annaghmore, Moy and Dungannon, and on to Donaghmore and Pomeroy, by teatime the train would eventually reach her destination, Carrickmore.

Her mother had relatives there and they had journeyed back and forwards to Belfast for years. In her teens, my grandmother played her fiddle with the best of them at music sessions in ceilidh houses across the countryside. The number of relatives decreased with each passing generation, yet friendships remained firm. When any of the Tyrone families attended the hospital or passed through Belfast, perhaps to go to work in England or further afield, they were always welcomed at my grandmother's home.

My mother stayed with a family she had known all her life. Mary and Bella, the two daughters of the house, were like sisters to my mother and my aunt. Every Friday night, having walked a quarter of the length of the road to Sixmilecross, or having got a lift with some of the local Gaelic footballers, they would be at a ceilidh up in the village they called 'Carmen', an abbreviation for the parish name, Termonmaguirc. They would dance the 'Waves of Tory' and 'Walls of Limerick' in the Patrician Hall. Afterwards she would return to the outshot bed, prepared for her beside the fire in the family's thatch-clad homestead.

Mick, who was like a surrogate father to her, was the dynamite man in charge of blasting at Carrickmore quarry. Like a lot of countrymen, he had two jobs, his first love being his tiny farm. On Saturdays she would bring food to Mick and the others digging on the bog or help with the animals. In her teens, she had been given a runt calf to tend and it would run to greet her like a pet. That evening they would all go to another ceilidh. It was an idyllic time, more like the screenplay of *The Quiet Man*, a chic dress sense and striking looks setting her apart from a lot of the locals.

Even after she left Orange's and started work, the Friday trip to Carrickmore, returning to Belfast on Sunday evening, would be part of the summer routine. In winter, weather permitting, the tradition somewhat reversed, the country girls coming to stay in the town, where they could enjoy the shopping, cinemas and, of course, big dance bands.

Gradually, going with boyfriends and future husbands, the frequency of the trips tailed off. My mother and father met at a dance in the Club Orchid. He was seven years older and when she would tease him from time to time about that he would laugh. 'I wasn't interested in this oul' lad,' she would say. They married a few years later, honeymooning in Killarney, where they acquired an enduring love of the west of Ireland. She earned more than him when then they were starting off. It never caused any tension. They never really worried about money in a material way, investing everything in family, friends and home. As long as they paid their bills, they were happy.

By all accounts, my father's mother, Sarah Ann, was formidable. She had spent her life in the mills, nursing her husband and taking care of her son. Forthright, nononsense in her ways, eyebrows raised when my mother and her new husband moved under the same roof as her. Against all the odds, the two women became incredibly close. The fact that my mother, having grown up in a big family, was an accomplished baker may have helped. Those who knew my grandmother certify that her cooking was distinctively lacking in flavour.

Before I was born, my mother had two miscarriages and almost died from an ectopic pregnancy. She emerged from hospital frail and gaunt. Helped by a friend, my grandmother doted, fussed and slowly nursed her back to her feet. My father made my mother drink a daily bottle of stout. 'It'll build you up,' he told her. Apart from an occasional glass of sherry at a wedding reception, it was the only alcohol she ever drank.

Her working life had started in a sheet metal works between Balmoral and Finaghy. She handled the payroll, bills and accounts. In those days, the site of the factory was out in the countryside with farms dotted nearby slowly coming under pressure from the urban sprawl along the main roads.

Often my mother went out for lunch, bringing buns or cakes she had baked to a relative who lived in a tiny row of bungalows just across the way. Joe McAfee worshipped his cousin, my other grandmother, turning to her regularly for counsel. Her approval of a girl he had met was the seal that led to marriage. He worked on the railways, the line running close to his home along the back of the engineering works. The kindest of individuals, Joe and his wife, Lily, were regular visitors to my grandmother's Falls Road home during that interlude following the war when, even in Belfast, religion did not seem to bear as much weight. Joe was from the Protestant wing of the family.

In the small firm, my mother loved the independence and camaraderie. A young boss with a taste for expensive and unusual automobiles somehow acquired a convertible once owned by the film star Rita Hayworth. He chauffeured my mother home to Cavendish Street.

'It conked out at the top of the Grosvenor Road,' she laughed. 'I was mortified. I tried to get out before anybody who knew me saw me, but naturally some of the local lads spied me in this big flashy car and they didn't let me forget it.'

She eventually left the engineering firm for a better job, her sister taking her place on her recommendation. My mother then worked for a couple of years in the Lord Mayor's Office in Belfast City Hall. Its copper-green dome crowns an imposing wedding cake building that is one of the focal points of the city's identity. Statues staring from the plinths around its grounds inscribe the names of dominance, industry and wealth: Harland, Pirrie, Dixon, Dufferin, McMordie.

My mother enjoyed the bustle. 'There was this feeling that because you were doing something for people it was more important work,' she said. She formed lifelong friendships.

Along with some colleagues, she applied for full civil service jobs when they were advertised by the motor tax office. An Englishman, who was the overall boss, and two local civil servants were on the interviewing panel. For the first time she encountered open sectarianism. Her recommendations were exemplary, her qualifications excellent and her performance strong; then came the question: 'What school did you go to?'

With her education at Orange's clear on the application, there could only be one reason for the query.

My mother was direct.

'I went to St Mary's and St Rose's and if you want to know my religion, I'm a Catholic.'

There was a fluster on the other side of the table. The civil servant who had posed the question perfunctorily assured her that her religion was of no consequence. She stood up and left, breaking into tears as she walked home.

To her surprise, she was called back to the motor tax office. Tentatively she knocked on the door of the Englishman's office and went inside.

'We are offering you the job Miss Toner.'

My mother was shocked. She stammered her thanks, him giving details of pay, outlining when she would start, having worked out her City Hall notice.

She was walking out again when he whispered in her ear, 'By the way Miss Toner, so am I.'

After that, on feast days and First Fridays, she would see him in St Malachy's, one of the city-centre Catholic churches, both exchanging knowing smiles at the memory of their first encounter.

The civil service pay and conditions were better but, under regulations, she had to leave when she married. It was as I started school that one of the bosses came up to Linden Street. The rules had changed. He implored her to come back. She and my father were looking at the new house and the money would help. My grandmother could look after me. They talked it over and agreed. My mother always joked that she had been employed twice in every place that she had worked. This was true. Each firm or office had always persuaded her to return for a while.

Back in the motor tax office, she moved up the scales to a supervisory role regularly dealing with members of the public. She thrived on the interaction. One day she was called to the counter. A minor detail had to be finalised. A tall man with a shock of slick black hair needed help with some details. He was most polite. She knew him right away. He was already building a firebrand reputation. She knew too some of his relatives in Tyrone, 'decent people'. A colleague attended one of his rallies out of curiosity. 'Maura,' he told my mother in the office on Monday morning, 'if I had met you or any other Catholic on the way out I would have killed them. That man's words are dangerous.'

My mother found this hard to reconcile with the polite individual waiting patiently at the counter. The young Ian Paisley went away, his licence stamped.

One night she returned home with a letter from a motorist from Crossmaglen. Driving without a disc for many years, he was objecting to the Newry police's suggestion that he should pay up. 'Do you not know,' he argued in the letter, 'we do not pay taxes in Crossmaglen?' My mother doubled over laughing at the way in which the individual was stating fact, as he knew it, trying to be helpful to the authorities.

The Troubles had their impact on her job. It was not only her having to walk the miles into town when the buses were off, it also brought her into direct contact with police. She was wary. Detectives were making regular requests. She insisted they follow procedure. The task of liaising with them was taken over by a boss.

She wanted me to take piano lessons. My father would stand on the Falls at the top of Broadway, waiting for me to emerge each Saturday morning. More often than not I would emerge after the lesson to find him talking to someone he knew. One Saturday he was approached by a stranger.

'Your wife works in the motor tax?'

My mother was always being asked to process last-minute paperwork for family, friends and neighbours. He replied that this was correct.

'She could help us,' the man said. My father realised this was not a typical request. He said nothing could be done, but the man said he would see him again. Soldiers shot dead the same IRA man two weeks later. My father recognised him from his picture in the paper.

Something changed in my mother the night we were put out of our home. It was not the material loss but rather the sheer shock of seeing so much threat to life and bloodshed. Now it would be called trauma. Then it was described as a breakdown. She was off work for a week. Friends from the motor tax office rallied around her. Nan Boyd sent a full, brand new set of tableware. Dorothy Thompson left off a box of groceries. Inside was an envelope with money. Both Protestants, they were her closest friends for thirty years until, distraught, she saw cancer claim them both.

There was no question, though, that after that night my mother was more cautious, less direct, not as adventurous. It did not help that, sitting across from the gas works and outside the better-protected commercial centre, her office was considered a target. Bomb scares became such a common occurrence that she and her colleagues hardly stirred. One afternoon the boss ran through the office. 'Get out. Get out. There's a bomb.'

My mother made it down from the third floor. Nan Boyd had been on the front desk when two men had walked in, stocking masks on, one with a gun and one who left a box in front of her on the counter. It exploded about ten minutes after they got out. Nan was shaking uncontrollably when my mother reached her and held her. The bomb blew a hole in the floor exactly where my mother's seat had been. The repairs took weeks. The staff continued to process licences behind lines of hardboard.

On Bloody Friday, my father was at home in the house at Hughes' Terrace because he was on night shift. Typically, he would get up around lunchtime and then go back to bed for a couple of hours in the evening before heading for work. The explosions must have started not long after two o'clock. By the time four or five had gone off, my father was putting on his coat.

'I have to make sure your mother is all right,' he told me when I suggested that he should not go. There was another explosion somewhere far away.

'Stay here son, or go to your granny's, but don't be going any further.' He was out the door and gone.

I stayed put for about five minutes. I thought I heard yet another explosion. I had heard bombs before, but never this many. I ran from the house to my grandmother's. The door was closed. That was unusual. The neighbours were standing outside, ears trained on the distance. I knew the McCormicks and they knew me.

'She went into town a couple of hours ago to pick up some fabric.'

My grandmother, I think, in her mind was still the twenty-year-old milliner and seamstress who prided herself on chalking out a dress pattern and sewing the garment on her Singer in no time at all. She was always picking up different types of cloth, always searching for usable remnants.

I knew my uncle and grandfather would be working. I tried not to show that panic was welling up inside. It had to be obvious. I started to run again.

'Where are you going son? You can wait here.'

'It's okay,' I shouted back, already heading towards the main road. 'It's okay.' I was telling it to myself as much as to Miss McCormick.

The crossroads on the Falls, where it was intersected by the Grosvenor and Springfield roads, was bordered on one side by shops and on the other by the hospital wall and Dunville Park. I once heard a soldier say that he would suffer anxiety attacks within a 500-yard radius of the junction. The open space created by the park allowed opportunities for those with guns, and a view of sorts towards the city centre. There was another explosion and then another and another as quick as that. I looked at the watch my father had given me for my First Communion. It was after three. Others stopped to look towards the city as well. I had watched similar scenes on television, but they were in far-off, hot places. The only way to describe this was as though the city was being attacked, under bombardment.

And it was.

It was the IRA. Nine were killed, more than 120 wounded.

I did not know that at the time. At the time, I thought many, many more would be dead. I must have heard ten explosions but there were more than double that number in all and not just in the centre, but even in the outskirts as people went about their lives and lost them on a Friday afternoon.

I was walking quickly now, along the hospital's high wall, down the Grosvenor Road towards the city. A steady stream of people flowed against me. One woman, her coat all dusty, was crying. 'Awful, just awful,' I heard her tell her companion.

On a man's forehead, there was a trace of caked blood.

There was another explosion, louder this time; it seemed to be at the far end of the Grosvenor, perhaps near the train station. I was at the back gate of the hospital now, with a clearer line of sight from the bend there towards town. I stopped. The stream had become a torrent, scores of people, all ages, alone and in groups, all hurrying. I debated turning back.

Just then, when there was no hope, I saw my mother. On the outside, nearest the road, my father had his arm around her shoulder and she was holding my grandmother's hand, their fingers interlaced around the handles of my grandmother's bag. They were together. I ran to them, springing with joy. At that point I cared nothing about the bombs, the smoke or the destruction. The three dearest people in my life were found.

'What are you doing here?' My father saw the relief on my face. There was no hint of chastisement. I saw the same relief in all three faces. They were pale, wide-eyed and breathing hard. I was unsure whether this was due to the uphill climb, their hurried strides or because of what they had experienced.

One blast was in Ormeau Avenue.

'We were going one way and a bomb went off, so we went the other way and a bomb went off there too,' my mother said.

Pure luck had brought the three of them together.

All of the people filing away from the city were jabbering their stories.

I cannot recall who suggested it, but after we turned the corner into Cavendish Street we went into St Paul's, kneeling briefly in prayer, enveloped by the church's coolness and silence, its darkness, familiarity and scent of burnt wax and stale incense.

We walked over to my grandmother's house. They watched the news with its horrific imagery.

'Poor, poor people,' said my grandmother.

'Fridays,' my mother said, as if uttering her innermost voice and casting from past to future, 'they'll never be the same again.'

Caught

Working for a firm designing telecommunications, everyone in the family acknowledged my uncle had 'brains to burn'. Still living at home with my grandparents, he travelled to England on occasion by plane, then a lifestyle that sounded much more glamorous than the reality of little hotels and bed and breakfasts used as accommodation for the training courses run by his company.

He loved every new technology, bringing home a Polaroid camera. We, my cousins and I, were stunned by pictures available in minutes. He bought a telescope through which we observed craters in the full moon. My grandmother was nervous that if the army raided they would think the tripod was for mounting a rifle. He came home with a hand-held electronic music box, though, try as we might, we could not reproduce the chords we heard on television adverts. Naturally, that did not stop us, forcing my grandmother after a couple of days to hide its batteries. I learnt chess on a magnetic board he bought in a shop in Birmingham, and for weeks we jockeyed for victory each night on a miniature pool table complete with spring-loaded cues that he found on his travels.

My uncle had vision too beyond the gadgetry, sitting at the kitchen table, soldering iron and fuse wire in hand, poring over some brittle circuit board. A while later there would be a dimming bulb on the ceiling at the top of the stairs and a double switch fixed where the old one had been next to the hallway door. He showed us mercury roll around his palm.

Different projects were undertaken without my grand-mother's knowledge. She said that for a while she never rightly knew what might happen when she would attempt to switch on a light.

At some stage, a fish tank appeared on the bookshelf next to the fireplace. I missed the books moved to the parlour. Amongst them were the works of Shakespeare, a family Bible, *Around the Boree Log*, *Betsy Gray or Hearts of Down*, *Holy War in Belfast* by the Protestant trade unionist Andy Boyd, and *The Capuchin Annual* of 1966 with its accounts of the Rising.

There were personal links to two books. *As I Roved Out* was written by a man called O'Byrne, who my grand-mother had known. Another uncle had taught in a school on the Whiterock Road where the principal was Michael McLaverty, the author of *Call My Brother Back*. It was my favourite. I read it, disbelieving almost that someone would find the place where I was growing up worthy of story. With the other books, it was a valued friend for an only child. Banishing them to the parlour would have been a hardship, except that the aquarium was the stuff of fresh imagination. I looked the word up in the dictionary, prac-tising spelling it because I knew it would be impressive if I included it in any class composition.

The first colour television I saw was in a house on my route home. Half a dozen of us pressed our noses against the window watching the saturated tones of a horse race until the owner emerged to shout at us to get away and then, for good measure, drew the curtains. I would have given anything to watch *The Undersea World of Jacques Cousteau* on the coloured television, yet the fish tank, all alive, brought that sense of exploration into the tiny living room of the two-up two-down.

At first, I hurried from school just to see if anything had changed. Extraordinary colours danced around the walls brightening them on the greyest day. My uncle had wired its lighting into position so that the tank sat flush on the shelf. Bubbles from an aerator concealed behind a mock toy castle gave movement to the water, gifting light across some big leafy plants. Plastic backing, simulating an underwater rockery fading into infinity, completed a mesmerising effect.

He brought me with him to the shop to buy stock. I stared in awe at the Lionfish, afraid to approach the glass in case their venom would render it porous. The colours were extraordinary. I relished the names: Butterfly Fish, Clownfish and Achilles Tang. My uncle had been reading. He had a freshwater tank and bought accordingly – Angel Fish, Black Mollies, Guppies and the Neon Tetra which would dart as if in shoal.

My grandmother complained about the space it took up, but she sat alongside me and watched the goings on, getting me to name the fish. The aquarium was a world of wonder. The greatest excitement came when the Guppies bred and a couple of dozen live little ones began swimming around the tank. I observed them almost in disbelief at their appearance. Their number reduced by the day. My uncle said the fitter were surviving. I believe he knew the adult fish were supplementing their diet with their young.

The fish tank was temporarily forgotten when he traded in his old car for a spacious new model. I think he was relieved to get rid of the Morris Minor. Only after he bought it at auction did filler holes in its passenger side become apparent. My mother, in the motor tax office, discovered the previous owner had been shot while driving to work.

Other uncles had families and their cars – Morris Oxfords, Hillman Imps and Ford Anglias – were small. Where they had an industrial quality, with starting handles, water splashing up through rusted floors and creaky wipers, this new Vauxhall was shiny and modern-looking, almost sporty. It was a passport to different places and the uncle would take us, his nephews, out to the countryside.

'Do you fancy a run?' That would be a question of a summer evening and we would already be fighting for the back-seat position. We coveted it because we thought perching on the armrest, which we would pull down to use as a seat, afforded its own superiority.

We did not know where we would end up. One night when he came in from work, a cousin said, 'You can't make it to Dublin and back.' We did. No motorways, bypasses or even dual carriageways; in those days Dublin was usually a four- or five-hour drive. We got out of the car in O'Connell Street, he bought us each a fish supper and we got back in for the return trip, arriving home to my grandmother's tut-tutting about two in the morning. Had his older sisters – our mothers – known, there would have been ructions. This enhanced our sense of daring.

Cousins stayed at my grandmother's house when it was too dangerous for them to cross the Ormeau Bridge in their school uniforms. There were 'Tartans' about then, sectarian gangs intent on violence. Addressing a big crowd in the park within earshot of my aunt's home just a few months earlier, a unionist politician spoke of 'liquidating' the enemy. The irony was that some of the lads, wearing their funny-bright chequered scarves, had played football with my cousins in that same park. My cousins stayed in my grandmother's for days on end, waiting for word that it was safe to be home. They were welcome company. Still, I found myself reading books and comics, for an only child learns to depend primarily on their own imagination.

I think my uncle consciously decided he wanted to remove us from the claustrophobic crush of the city. By taking us away from the greyness and smoke permeating the night air, he recaptured part of his own youth, rediscovering the forests and fields around Belfast. From the Antrim shoreline, we saw the sun set across Lough Neagh. We ran from a little pier back to the car as a cloud of midges descended. We walked by the Lagan from Shaw's Bridge up to Hilden and he pointed out darting kingfishers, wagtails and moorhens. We climbed Cave Hill to watch from Napoleon's Nose and McArt's Fort the evening tide workings of the port. Along the way, we heard stories of Dean Swift, the slumbering inspiration for Gulliver, and Henry Joy and the gathering of the United Irishmen before their ill-fated 1798 uprising. At the top, we ate sandwiches prepared by my grandmother and chocolate bars the uncle had bought in the little shop on the corner of Violet Street before we left. When it was time to leave, we skittled down the sharpest gradient, slipping and sliding on pebbles rounded like marbles by the dry summer.

My favourite place was to the southwest of the city below Colin, a low rolling hill.

My grandmother owned two or three fields in a fold on the slopes. Entwined in family history, bequeathed by some long-dead relative, they were worth nothing monetarily. Access land-locked, the fields had been unfarmed since the war years. A one-man tracked tractor, a monument to those times, was decaying into the ground.

During the war, my mother had attended school up the hill in the Orange Hall at Castlerobin. The cottage where the family had escaped the threat of the Blitz had been turned to rubble by cattle, the elements and time. At the top field, after playing for hours, we lay on a big iron cover, installed by the water board, to feel cooled by the sheer volume rushing through the well. Once, we prized the cover open and were almost overcome by the roar of chill air pushed up from the darkness.

It was neither the cottage nor the fields which held fascination for us as children, but the shaded glen and its stream running through its stepping stones. It was there I saw my first fox, auburn and white through the undergrowth, quick and away; there that I fell in a river for the first time; there I netted frogspawn in jam jars and, wearing shorts, encountered the unpleasant novelty of a nettle bed. Yet early on a summer evening, when shafts of a setting sun sent shafts of light through the foliage, it was a place of beauty where leprechauns, legends and fairy thorns could easily be familiars.

Revisiting boyish skills, his shirtsleeves rolled up, my uncle showed us how to fish by hand. As he leaned over the stream's bank at a knowing spot, he said salmon would have been there in the past whereas now it might be rainbow trout. We watched as his concentration focused. Above the silty bank, he became silent, arm hardly moving, us all poised on tiptoes, staring, staring into the glare on the water.

'Wooow.' All at once he splashed out a bow of water.

We ran and jumped, catching his exhilaration. And there it was, flapping, all silvery-black like a dagger on the grass. We stared at the trout, to my eyes more exotic than the species in the tropical fish shop, for I had seen it plucked live from its home place and exposed. My uncle lifted the trout gently, putting it in a big jar he filled with stream water. We took turns carrying it back across the fields, holding it gingerly in the car, peering close-up at the fish through the magnifying glass.

None of us questioned then that we should do that, uproot it, make it ours, isolate it, take it home. Back at my grandmother's my uncle softly put the jar into the aquarium to allow the temperature to even. After a couple of hours, he released the trout into the tank where it darted, wild, up and down the glass.

Only my grandfather voiced concern. 'You shouldn't have done that,' was all he said.

I watched it over the following weeks, noticing it still moved in flicks, agitated when anyone cast a shadow across the glass. Measuring more than the span of my fingers when first installed, its belly colour was not dissimilar to the Angel Fish and Black Mollies swimming alongside. In certain light only, the rainbow between silver and black glinted blue and emerald, reminding me of how it looked, gawping, when first taken from the stream. It grew. It was clear it would become too big for the tank. The other fish seemed intimidated by its increasing feral ferocity. I put myself in its black eyes, brash electric between the plants, rocks and other hazards. Most of all, though, the boundaries of the tank seemed to encroach on the trout's very essence.

I got up for school, sitting as usual beside the aquarium to tie my shoes. Noticing water drops on the lino floor, I looked into the tank. I looked for the trout. It was gone. I was afraid. I had watched my grandfather in the backyard take newborn kittens and hold them in a bucket of water until life was gone. I had struggled to balance this action with his kindness to his grandchildren, his smile. He walked into the room, no trace of deceit.

'Where is it?' I asked.

'It had to go,' he replied.

'Where, where?'

He saw I was vexed.

'It's okay, he took it back where it belongs.'

My uncle had left for work an hour earlier. I heard the car start outside, impressed that the ignition had turned over at the first attempt on a morning where a frost filigreed the window corners. On his way to work, he told me, he had stopped at the Waterworks, a big holding reservoir in the north of the city, and there he had released the trout from the big plastic bag full of water that had been contained in a box in the car's passenger well. The Waterworks was another location we would visit of an evening, usually as autumn came and we could not venture so far out of the city's limits. I never went there or passed it again without thinking of the trout, its black dorsal indistinguishable

from the murky shades of the reservoir, it flashing through
the water as quicksilver unhindered, the first and last fish
my uncle ever caught for us.

Arm

The first thing I saw was the blood. His face, normally, if anything, slightly ruddy, was bleached. He was sitting in the back room, his shirt half off, when I came down at breakfast time. Dangling by his side, the empty sleeve was saturated. His right arm was red with blood. My mother came in, fussing with dressings. My father was just in from the night shift. He smiled at me.

'Don't worry, I'm okay.'

I always worried when my father went out to work at night.

Soon after we had to leave our house, he left his job in James Mackie & Sons, the engineering works just up the road from where we were now living. He had started there before the war, the Second World War. A factory that once transported huge textile machines around the globe switched to a war footing and made Mills bombs, munitions machines and weapon parts. It took on as many workers as possible, even Catholics. A fellow apprentice contacted my father years later. He wrote: 'The war years were the happy times.' My father was amused by the irony. There is a picture of him then, standing alongside another lad in front of a machine, both in overalls. He must have been about eighteen, a full head of hair, a full smile and not a care.

My father, I gathered, had some run-ins with 'the office', who refused to recognise his or any other union. He was the informal spokesman for the others, once threatening bosses that his entire department would strike if a man unfairly sacked was not given his job back. Within hours the man was reinstated.

An environment as hard as its machines, it was an inhospitable place for a boy from the Falls, even though his home was only a half mile away, even though the foundry itself sat within Catholic west Belfast. Beaten for being left-handed to the point he became ambidextrous, he had been bright in a school where teachers tended to notice only the sons of bookmakers, publicans and doctors. He went into Mackie's at the age of fourteen when his father, the grandfather I never knew, was stricken by a heart complaint. It was a sudden start. Soon after, religion discovered, there were fist fights. My father never made it any secret, going on to help organise an annual weekend retreat for Catholic workmates. They were always in the minority. None ever became a shop-floor foreman. There was tension in the background, mainly in July. On the Friday before the Twelfth Fortnight, an Orange parade took place around the factory yard, pictures of the British Queen and union flag bunting were draped across the machines. Catholic workers would fidget sullenly by their machines waiting for the release of the horn.

For all that, my father was ingrained in Mackie's. He met the best of people there, he said, and had a loyalty to the place and his workmates, playing alongside some of them in the firm's football team. In his mid-twenties he contracted tuberculosis, probably from the damp city, damp fog, damp house. His mother watched a priest administer the Last Rites to her only child. He was treated in the tin huts left after the war by the Americans at Musgrave Park

Hospital, a patient of the new health service. He lost part of a lung and others died around him. The husband of a cousin visited every week to shave him. Gradually he recovered sufficiently to climb out a window at the back of the hut to go to dances at nearby Balmoral with some of his nurses. A Mackie's boss visited my grandmother, telling her not to be concerned, that the job would be there no matter how long the wait. Peter Paisley was good to his word. Over a year later my father resumed his place at his machine, a homecoming.

He was trusted there, one of two self-taught eye doctors in the Faller Shop. In a factory where wages were measured by piecework, men could not afford to take time to go to hospital when a fleck of hot metal flashed into their eye. My father would wet a matchstick with spit to use to roll up the lid. Then, with a hand as steady as any surgeon, he used the point of a needle to deftly pick the metal off the eyeball.

The Troubles exposed Mackie's sinews. My father continued to collect pools money every week, another important role in a place where the only hope of escape might be in the imagination of a big win. The numbers came up for a neighbouring department's syndicate. There was jubilation until it emerged that their collector, instead of turning in the coupons, had been pocketing the money. Afterwards, every Friday night the foreman reached him his pay packet and, without a word, two men waiting by his machine would take the envelope from his hand, open it and extract a share of the money for distribution to the cheated men. This happened every Friday night for years. A few of the fifty or so in my father's department told the others they would be taking over the collection, that they did not want a Catholic collecting their money. That week forty-five men handed their money as usual to my father.

A friend from the Shankill warned him about a new apprentice.

'Do you know who he is?'

My father truthfully replied that he did not.

The friend mentioned a surname, a surname subsequently synonymous with a loyalist paramilitary group killing Catholics.

'They're a bad crowd. You watch yourself, Jim,' the friend said.

'He does his work,' my father told him. 'And as long as he does that I'll treat him the same as the rest of them.' My father showed the lad how to run the Faller Shop's mightiest machines. He followed my father like a dog. 'He couldn't have been better, eager to please, pity he went the way he did,' my father would say later. 'He'll have to answer to his God.'

The friend who warned him about the apprentice had a brother killed by the IRA. The brother had been on the fringe of a mob stoning Catholic homes. One of those who had tried to hijack the pools collection rattled a tin under my father's nose. On it had been scribbled and taped a card: 'Loyalist Widows'. The floor went quiet, Catholics and Protestants alike watching what my father would do. It was a calculated attempt to insult, humiliate, dominate.

My father put his hand in the pocket of his dungarees to pull out a few coppers.

The man was surprised. 'I didn't think you would give to this,' he said.

'Loyalist widows?' said my father. 'Sure there couldn't be enough of them.'

There was a face-off with spanners drawn. The man was pulled away, still shouting invective.

My father went to the funeral on account of his friend, blending anonymously with mourners, some in the black leather coats and dark glasses already associated with loyalist paramilitarism.

When his friend returned to work, he approached my father at his machine.

'I heard what they did, Jim, with the tin. It was none of my doing. I've told them they shouldn't have done that. I'm sorry.'

'You have nothing to apologise for,' my father told him and that was it, friendship firm still.

When we were put out of our house the same friend approached again. 'How much do you need?' He pulled out a bundle of notes, every penny he could muster. My father refused the offer; he never forgot the kindness.

It was a wrench to leave Mackie's. He sat a test for the new firm in the chaos of us having no home.

'It was easy if you knew anything about machines,' he said.

Mackie's success led to its redundancy. Machines it sent east were being copied overseas. Cheap synthetics and other fabrics were being sent back west. Old industry in Belfast was dying. Autolite was new. Making the components for Ford's carburettors, it was subsequently taken over by the American automobile giant.

In Mackie's, a man who had lost a leg in the war would hit the doors of the stalls with his stick to rouse anyone spending too long in the toilets. At Autolite the bosses negotiated with my father's union, the Transport and General. It was allowed to meet openly and recruit. My father said he thought he had arrived in a holiday camp. For the first couple of weeks he wore the new, blue, shiny nylon overalls, soon reverting to his more comfortable Mackie's cotton dungarees.

The production-line had problems when he arrived. New carburettors were moulded in separate halves. When bonded, fine holes had to align to ensure the carburettors worked. Too often drills were breaking inside the moulds. Machines were turning out ever-growing piles of scrap. Only my father's machine was hitting quotas. The bosses came to watch him. Eventually, one asked what he was doing differently. He was working the same machine, he was using the same parts from the die-cast department, he had the same drills, yet he was turning out hardly any scrap. He explained to them that their drills would never work. The drills were the finest available, they said, imported from Germany. Yes, my father told them, 'but they're not sharpened the Mackie's way'. From that afternoon he had a new job sharpening the bits, judging every one by eye and with thirty-two years of Faller Shop experience. Before they went back to their office, he asked the bosses why whole carburettors were being scrapped when only one half was faulty. These university-taught engineers scratched their heads and, later that day, issued a memo to foremen in the Kingsberry section telling them to only discard defective halves. From that day productivity rose.

The shifts and the location of the factory were the main problems with the new job. Sited on the edge of

Andersonstown, alongside the motorway, the factory was about four miles away from our temporary home, Harry's house on the Springfield Road. The shifts rotated in three-week patterns; 'the early' week from 7 a.m. to 3 p.m., then the 3 p.m. until 11 p.m., and finally the night shift week from 11 p.m. until 7 a.m. The money was better but the shifts were difficult to get used to, at first, for a man who had worked the 'nine to five' in Mackie's. It would have been testing in ordinary times. These were not ordinary times.

During rioting, the first thing burned would be buses. Services were sometimes suspended for days. This was before a few local men imported London cabs to pack in passengers and ply around the Falls barricades. Often then my father would have to walk, through Beechmount, out onto the Falls, then up the Andersonstown Road and down Finaghy Road North.

Dangerous shifts were those finishing and starting at 11 p.m., darkness in Belfast rarely a friend. Some nights, when he knew there was going to be trouble, depending on whether it was the start or finish of a shift, my father would either set out early or would not come home. These times he would then stay with relatives living down the road from Autolite. There a settee was folded out into a bed. It was the only large piece of furniture my parents salvaged from our home. There was no room for it in the new accommodation, so they gave it to family and, when my father needed, he slept on that couch that had come from our home.

The night my father was bloodied, some loyalist leader in the east of the city declared war on the British army. It was a Friday night shift, the worst because it shortened the weekend. He set out early, leaving my mother and myself at my grandmother's, around the corner from Harry's house. Everyone listened to each radio bulletin then to hear what was happening in neighbouring communities, distant streets and alien territory. Tension crackled across the city like static electricity. My mother and I walked home; a bonus for me in losing the house that I could stay full-time with my parents.

It must have been early autumn, perhaps September, for the yellowy-brown was on the trees stretching up the wide pavement in front of Hughes' Terrace. It must have been before nine o'clock, for the light was just turning to gloom, the Springfield Road deserted.

We turned from Crocus Street and were about thirty yards up the road when the firing came. Word had it a few days later that it was a Bren gun used by the IRA from Clonard. Whoever was firing was not experienced. Far too long to be controlled, even I knew this was an inexpert burst. Perhaps a finger jammed on the trigger, or maybe the sheer vibration held it fast. The effect was to spit bullets everywhere; some of them neon red tracers. A few must have been close, for I felt the air punched two or three times as if balls were flying past my ear. The target was Springfield Barracks back down the road behind us. It is doubtful any struck home. There was no return fire. My mother and I instinctively cleaved to the pavement behind a tree. I noticed some fresh fallen leaves and recoiled from some dog dirt just ahead of us. When the firing paused, we rolled our way across to the door of Harry's house, her reaching up from her knees to put the key in the lock before dragging me inside. We sat in the back room, breathing heavily.

My mother never cursed, but she had angry words for the trainee gunner: 'The UDA declares war on the army and the IRA does the fighting.' She hissed as though speaking at normal level might attract more bullets. We lay on the floor through that night, firing intensifying, intensifying, intensifying, until it became a constant.

'Say a prayer your father's okay,' my mother told me. Saying Hail Marys was the Catholic counting of sheep. I drifted to sleep, 'Hail Mary Full of Grace', the pings and whines receding.

Just after dawn she wakened me. The shooting was over. I went upstairs to chilled sheets and slept again. Later, I heard the hall door open, my father's voice and a yell from my mother.

I went downstairs, no clue as to why mother had yelled, and found him there, sitting, bleeding drips from his right arm onto the floor. I looked at the clock. It was half seven. A workmate had given him a lift home.

My mother dressed the raggedy gory track that ran from the muscle on his upper arm all the way down to his wrist. She cleaned it with water just cooled from the kettle, then dabbed the length of it with cotton wool soaked in an antiseptic wash. He hardly winced. She wound the bandage around his arm.

He briefly told us what had happened. He had been walking past the shops near St James' when an armoured car swung on to the Donegall Road. It is a long road, split by the motorway, traversing very republican and very loyalist areas.

'Somebody opened up.'

That was another phrase you would hear a lot, 'opening up'. Back then it did not mean sharing emotions, describing instead anything from a few shots loosed off recklessly right the way through to a full-scale ambush. On this occasion, rifle-fire hit the armoured car, which in turn sprayed bullets from its machine gun. My father was lucky to be near a low wall. He took cover as bullets blew out a line of holes in the brickwork above him. I saw that the left shoulder of the dungarees, which he was still half wearing, was peppered with red-brown dust.

I thought of the wound on my grandfather's arm. This was not the same.

'Were you shot?'

'No son, I wasn't shot.' My father laughed. 'I was hurt in work.'

Still shivering from the near miss, he had punched in his time card. That night his concentration was elsewhere. He was shaking as he used the grinding machine with its whirring wheels, sparks and deafening noise. Its protective guard had been removed to allow easier access. His right sleeve caught on the rotor, dragging him into the machine. Had he hesitated he would have lost the arm, possibly his life. The cotton sleeve tore, giving him the second he needed to reach with his left hand and hit the stop button. Had he been wearing the nylon overalls they would not have ripped. The Mackie's dungarees saved him.

The injury healed over a couple of weeks, but the scar remained. I would see it sometimes when he might roll back his sleeve in summer, a long ugly raised line of dead white tissue mapping a jagged road the length of his arm.

For close to half a century he worked at the machines of Mackie's and Ford. He was not once late for work in all that time, not once; on all those shifts, on any of those nights, through gunfire and past bombs, during all those Troubles.

Windows

Playing hide and seek with cousins in a tiny terrace house was never a good idea. Sitting under a table, knocking its leg, I brought down a whole leaf upon which plates, cups and saucers had been placed. The crockery smashed over the floor, all tiny, jagged pieces, a complete dinner set complete no more. I ran from the house.

Hours later, when I returned, it had been swept.

'Never mind,' my grandmother said. 'Sure, we can replace plates, can't we?'

Her tolerance made me feel worse.

She let me away with things never allowed in her own children. Tough in ways on her daughters, sons and in-laws, she doted on me, waiting at the parlour window each day to see me return from school at lunch and in the afternoon.

She defended me ferociously, right, wrong or even uncertain.

Around a half dozen of us one day were playing outside, a game we called a-rally-o. We chased each other ruthlessly, harmlessly, running around the business of the street.

It was an otherwise quiet afternoon. There were no soldiers about. A horse-drawn cart clicked along, the man with the reins occasionally shouting, 'Any oul' rags?' He showed as little enthusiasm as his rickety horse. A couple of the street dogs ignored the piebald to join us in our game.

A man rounded the corner from the square almost bumping into one of my friends. He let out a roar, throwing his walking stick spinning at shin height. It clattered the lad's ankles and he yelped in pain. Without further commentary, the man retrieved his blackthorn and went on his way. He came from the far end of the street, impossible to mistake because, incredibly bow-legged and flat-footed, he did not so much walk as waddle. I fancied he might have been angry at the sight of us running unchecked. I was outraged with all of a ten-year-old's venom and viciousness.

Waiting until he became a distant dot and stretching for all the power I could muster, I yelled: 'Duck feet.'

It does not sit well on the page because when I shouted I extended both words. 'Duuuuckkk feeeeeeet.' Carrying for five or six seconds, the insult travelled like a gunshot on the breeze. At first jubilant for raising my voice against his tyranny, I noticed the dot become bigger and bigger again. This man, who had no call that I could see to be angry in the first place, had turned and was coming back. My friends looked at him then me. I looked at him then them. We scattered.

I ran into the house, straight upstairs. Choking back an instinct to shelter beneath the bedclothes, I hovered at the top of the landing. There I ensured I could hear and not be seen.

My grandmother, as usual, was in the scullery. About three minutes later, there was a knock on the door.

'Hello?' I heard her say.

'Somebody here, somebody here called me a name.' The man was jabbering, not quite coherent. To me he sounded as though his face was red.

My grandmother was perplexed.

'What? Somebody called you what?'

'Duck feet,' he said.

More confused, I think, she seemed to conclude he was a malcontent. At least in the round, in my opinion, this was correct. I could not see but imagined her drawing herself up to her full height of five feet four.

'Nobody here called you anything. Now on you go. Go on or I'll be getting my husband.'

I thought of my grandfather, the most gentle of individuals.

Confronted by my grandmother, formidable in every way, the man thought better of his position.

'I thought he was here.'

'There's nobody here but me, but my husband and son will be home soon.'

Because she had the radio on in the kitchen when I yelled, and had neither heard nor seen me come in, she was adamant, sufficient to make him doubt he had the right house. Tiptoeing into the bedroom, peering from behind the curtain, I saw him stand on the pavement and momentarily scratch his head while examining neighbouring houses. At one point, his shoulders sagged and off he went. He had given up on the notion of bringing the culprit to justice, while I, of course, felt justice had been done.

Pressing closer to the window, I watched him rock and roll back down the street. My grandmother never mentioned the encounter at the door and I knew better than to broach the subject.

She was back in the kitchen. I could hear her lilting one of her favourites, 'Eileen Og'. She broke off mid-sentence to turn up the volume on the radio. This was an hourly observance. For two or three minutes she listened reverentially, lamenting on the riots, shootings and bombings reported from across the city.

'Jesus, Mary and Joseph,' she would say when she was particularly shocked, if someone was hurt or killed.

The radio had a place of honour in the house, though not quite on the same level as the little crafted wooden altar that framed the Sacred Heart picture and its blinking neon lamp. She must have listened to every news bulletin. In times of tension, around the ever-growing number of anniversaries, parades and flashpoints, she might bring the radio in to the living-room table, sitting by it, tuning the dial ahead of time.

At night, it would be a companion in the bedroom. Sometime after midnight, the BBC would give itself over to jazz music, something we both detested; my grandmother because there was no more news, me because it would keep me awake if she had dozed off, as she occasionally did, before transmission ended.

My bed was at the window over the front door, theirs on the other side of the big room, headboard to the interior wall. My uncle slept in the back room, where he had managed to build a stand-alone shower, complete with electric water heater. This was real innovation for houses in the early seventies where the norm was still an outside toilet at the far end of the yard.

The nightly routine was the same no matter what; my grandmother listening to the radio, my grandfather kneeling by the bed to say his rosary. I loved nights when it rained, tracking little rivulets down the window until they became a stream flowing into an imaginary river every bit as real as the Amazon or Nile we had traced in school.

In the background, a voice recited the shipping forecast: Viking, Forties, Cromarty, Forth and Tyne, Dogger, Fisher, German Bight and Humber. I had no clue where these were but loved the lyrical quality to the plummy accent. The cadence reminded me of the litany of saints intoned in Clonard's benediction. I listened out in particular for Fastnet, Irish Sea, Rockall and Malin. My uncle had told me these were around our shores. On stormy nights in shapes on the pane, I could see little trawlers ply through the great wave. Rain after dark meant there rarely was shooting. I concluded that people with guns wanted to avoid getting them rusty. In the corner, my grandfather's catarrh would gradually subside into wheezy snores. Usually, after I drifted to sleep, often with a cat purring beside me, my grandmother turned off the radio.

For all her addiction to the news and her many stories of her youth, never did I hear her express a political opinion beyond a 'tut tut'. Her priority only was family and their protection. When the Troubles touched, as when we were put out of our home, she shrugged as if to indicate this was part of Belfast's weather. She got on with making sure there was food on the table, turning the mangle before putting washed and wrung clothes on the line in the back yard, and stitching the knees of the trousers I routinely tore at school.

As she grew older, she talked more about the past.

Born in the family home in north Belfast, she had trained as a milliner and dressmaker. Well into her sixties, I marvelled at her chalking a pattern outline onto a piece of fabric. She would then skim along the lines with her scissors, every bit as expert as my grandfather taking his knife to a meat joint. She knew all the measurements. Running repairs to my school trousers and sewing back shirt buttons were an exception, her work overwhelmingly designed for the women in the family, her daughters, granddaughters and occasionally herself.

I studied as she scrutinised her sewing machine, threading needle, stringing a matching thread to the bobbin. She might turn the wheel by hand a few times then, gently at first, she eased on the foot pedal, setting the Singer off at a rate of knots. She pulled the material through, sewing an even seam. In an hour or so she placed a finished blouse, dress or jacket on a coat hanger, standing back to admire the overall effect.

When not sewing, she stood for hours baking in the tiny scullery, apple and sponge cakes, meat pies and rolls. If the notion took her, she would experiment, frying thin crisps better than any of the mass-produced packets and baking mint sweets in irregular little balls. She loved special occasions, making us flip pancakes on Pancake Tuesday and, at Hallowe'en, burying in an apple cake a sixpence folded inside greaseproof paper. She always somehow made sure I got the slice with the coin.

Around dinnertime each evening, when anyone was not home, she became more agitated, pacing between the scullery's steaming pots and hissing pans and the parlour window. There she tugged at the curtains, looking along the street for my uncle or grandfather.

As time ticked through her day, rarely did she take much of it for herself.

She went perhaps once fortnightly into the city centre, this usually to pick up fabric, wool or thread that she could not get nearby. The shops around the Springfield and Falls junction were her main outing. She stopped, chatting to neighbours and shopkeepers. A trip to pick up a few groceries could thus take a couple of hours, me often alongside taking all in.

'How are you Mrs Toner?' one would ask.

'Och I'm all right. How are you?'

They would discuss ailments of the body and ailments of the times.

'Terrible isn't it?'

'It is so it is. This place'll never get better so it won't – too much hate.'

In the evening, she seldom ventured out, although one of my earliest memories was of her taking me into town, meeting my mother after she had finished work and all three of us going to a café. After eating, we went to the Avenue picture house to see *The Sound of Music*. My child's eye retains the abiding impression of glittery lights everywhere, a musky smell of perfume, ice cream in a tub eaten with a little wooden spoon, and the rich velvet reds of the big curtains and seats.

My grandmother was as much in awe as me.

'Sure, it was wonderful,' she said as we left.

My mother later told me there were doubts on whether to go. Apparently, my grandmother was not happy reading that Julie Andrews left convent life for Alpine yodelling. The last film she had been to the cinema to see had been *The Song of Bernadette*. When it came to the musical, the catchy score swung things in favour of the Von Trapps.

My grandmother went out another night to watch me take to the stage, my only appearance at St Paul's feis. Not being able to sing and never having liked Irish reels or jigs was no obstacle. There was a recital or, as I called it at the time, a 'rectal'. Cued by a teacher I walked on stage. The lad before me had delivered a poem about going up airy mountains and down rushy glens. I started well, playing on my fiddle in Dooney, folk dancing like waves on the sea: Yeats.

I stared at people staring back at me. In a row midway down the hall I saw my grandmother flanked by my parents, unmistakable in her little fur hat. She had given it to me to sooth my jaw when I lay sick in bed. I thought of the mumps. My mind went as blank as the faces in the audience. Skipping whole stanzas, I stammered out a couple more lines from somewhere near the end of the poem and ran off. People applauded, hesitantly, out of sympathy not appreciation.

'Sure, most of them don't know that poem anyway,' she told me afterwards. 'Never you mind. It was a big thing to get up there.'

She had performed herself, years earlier. Trained as a classical violinist by an aunt, she was more comfortable playing the fiddle with traditional musicians at dances and ceilidhs across west Tyrone. Her style, looks and feistiness made her popular.

'I see you are not in uniform yourself?' she told one man in Tyrone who had lamented how few locally were serving in the war.

She lived through two world wars, the Easter Rising, partition of the country and the creation of two new states. She knew history first-hand.

Her father, a joiner, led a squad in the Belfast shipyard when the keels were laid for the *Titanic* and the other great vessels of the White Star Line. In 1912, he fled from the shipyard with hundreds of Catholics. It was called a pogrom, another in a series to enter nationalist folklore to add to the sense of grievance. Less well known was that hundreds of pro-Home Rule Protestants were also chased by their co-religionists stoked to violence by industrialists, politicians and the Orange Order.

Her grandfather had actually been Protestant, converting after meeting a girl from an influential Catholic family on the slopes of Colin Glen. His family, the Christians, settled in the area when they arrived from the Isle of Man. For two centuries or more, they were buried in the Church of Ireland graveyard near Derriaghy. Like so many others, their children moved into the new city's textile and ship-building industries and started families.

My grandmother was one of four, three daughters and a son; a sister, Lucy, died from pneumonia. She met her husband, my grandfather, at the funeral of a friend of both families. Dainty and petite, Jeannie Christian captured James Toner with her eyes. They were an unlikely pair, he the strong, raw country lad, an immigrant into the town, a family-trained butcher who could kill a cow with a bolt gun, have it skinned and cut into joints for sale in the shop in no time at all.

A regular at concerts and recitals, Jeannie had command of an oral trove of stories passed from generation to generation. She recounted, with an effortless focus, tales as pictured in her mind of the byways of Belfast and her family townland beyond. The main history that attracted my grandfather was the form guide of *The Irish News* racing pages. Over two things, politics and losing horses, he could be gruff. For her, his children and grandchildren, he had only the most open smile and a wink.

Cavendish Street, at the right money in the right area, was their first home. Her father made the wooden altar. Five children, two girls then the boys, arrived in quick succession. Her sister, Nellie, working in Gallagher's tobacco factory, lived with them, helping raise the family. I never knew her. She died in the 1950s. Cancer.

My grandfather had recovered fully from his own wound by the time they married. The same year that he was shot, my grandmother lost her favourite uncle to a bullet. Official records put Paddy McKenna dying in the Mater Hospital. Some accounts say he was hit in the stomach, sitting on a window sill. The way she told it, he was hit at the door of her Lepper Street home. Teasing back the lace curtain, she watched him approach from the window, then walked out into the hallway that July day in 1921 to greet him. Random fire had been traded all that month across Belfast's sectarian lines, always present, sometimes invisible and frequently deadly. That same day, republicans shot and killed a Protestant girl near the Markets district. She was fourteen. When Paddy McKenna was hit by a unionist sniper's bullet, blood, bone and brain matter spattered over my grandmother.

She had a dress on that day. She had just made it and was trying it on for the first time. She ran to her uncle, desperately attempting to staunch an unstoppable wound, other relatives and neighbours panicking and frantic around her for the futility. She always told of what had happened as though it was still happening.

Half a century later, my grandfather sometimes rolled up the sleeve of his shirt exposing the big gouge left by the dum-dum. Long since it had ceased to cause him physical pain, but the sight of it seemed to mesmerise my grandmother. She might stop what she was doing before softly placing a hand on his shoulder.

'There, there,' she would say, perhaps tearing a thread at the side of her cardigan absent-mindedly with her other hand. I would watch her gaze retreat to the wooden altar, still off somewhere trying to heal a wound.

Bullets do not just travel in distance. They travel through windows in time.

Shooting

My uncle went to the funeral of this man he did not know. No one, save me, understood why.

I see his silhouette, forty years ago, still caught between the wipers. I heard the thump on the bonnet and my uncle's foot punch the brake.

His face was on the windscreen, his eyes staring, bulging in fear.

My uncle wound the window down. The man was right there.

'Get me to hospital. I've been shot. I've been shot.'

He repeated it as though trying to convince himself.

We had dropped off my father at Mass and I was still in the back seat of the little car. I stayed put. He stumbled round the front, clinging as if afraid my uncle would drive off, taking his life away. The passenger door was open. He threw himself into the seat and, with his scream, we were moving.

The hospital, the Royal, was a couple of miles away. I knew every brick on our route. We were already passing the scrap yard, Eastwood's. Beyond, the three great western roads in the city, the Andersonstown, the Glen and Falls flowed into a confluence marked by the triangle of cemetery, bus depot and barracks.

'Ah Christ, no.'

The car hit the ramps at the barracks and the chicane outside the cemetery faster than its suspension could cushion. I saw him shudder. I glanced at Milltown's gates.

I always associated that place with tension, for on the few occasions when I was brought to funerals, there were mumbled prayers and cold and tears. Voluntarily going to such a place seemed strange to a child, so much misery. Even curiosity at the sallow faces could not hold me there and I fidgeted always to be away. Passing those gates always brought a little ice, winter or summer.

'Aw Christ. It hurts. It hurts.'

I studied the back of his head, concentrating on the engine to avoid hearing his words pitch to screams. I looked out of the window to my left. There were the long railings of the park. Somewhere through the dark, I imagined its bowling green, bandstand and open-air swimming cooler, all swept this night by rain and empty of the joy of people.

Then the way became bordered by the Protestant cemetery, some headstones smattering back glints of light, each one a death's reminder. I had to look back into the car, forced to stare again at the back of his head.

I glanced down at my knees. They were shaking.

After the junction with the Whiterock came a whole crush of shops. On Sundays, when my father would walk me to a football match at Casement Park, we would go into a little sweet shop there and he would buy me a bag of lemon drops or chewy bon bons dusted with sugar icing. The 'lion house' was on the right, imposing with its ornamental gateposts and statues guarding its door. My parents would point to it from the bus when I was younger. 'There's the lion house.' I knew the black stone lions would be watching from their pedestals, judging my fear.

'Jesus, Jesus stop the car. It hurts. It hurts. Ah Jesus.'

'Where are you hit?'

My uncle asked the question in the most matter-of-fact way imaginable. I think he was perhaps asking to stop the man's screams and if that was so, it worked. The man paused. I saw his shoulders ease and he looked at my uncle, as if wanting to help both of them somehow comprehend the enormity of what had transpired.

'The stomach. He shot me in the stomach.'

I was ten. I could easily distinguish gunshots, the crack of pistols, the machine tat-tat-tat of automatics, roars of the big rifles. I already knew a stomach wound from any gun, even a little one, could end life, could put you in Milltown. I had already witnessed wounds. As we tumbled from a bus, I saw a man's body lifted into the ambulance. There was a horrible mess around his head, all white and black redness and a lifeless arm seemed to loll back towards his van as the ambulance sped off, its doors still open. A bomb was thrown into the chip shop, so close it had broken our windows. I went outside and saw the bloody-messed bandages and people with bright blood flowing from heads and hands. There was the fleshy hole on my grandfather's arm, so big I could bury two fingers inside. I had asked him once if it had hurt. He said it had not, that it was numb and that he had run like a rabbit chased by foxes.

This man was deep in pain, scared, terrified, no question. In the darkness, there was the smell of wet sweat. There was steam coming from his head. He said he was a chef in another hospital and had been on his way home. Because he was walking towards Andersonstown, they knew he was Catholic.

We were passing the 'Giant's Foot', an undeveloped sprawl of a track we would use as a shortcut if there was trouble on the road. That was the phrase everyone used: 'trouble on the road'. It covered everything from rioting and burning cars to shooting and gun battles. It occurred to me that this night we were the 'trouble on the road'. I saw no other person. There was just the three of us.

Beechmount, a residential home for the elderly run by nuns, sat back in several stepped acres of land. Each autumn we would venture the wrath of its groundsman by hunting under the sprawling chestnut trees for conkers to string, smash and batter each other's knuckles.

'He just shot me. It was the pillion passenger on a motorbike. He just shot me. Ah Christ, it hurts.'

There was another smell, metallic almost, like the spirals of drilled aluminium that would cling to my father's overalls. Blood. I did not need to see it to know the smell. It was like the time the football had hit me square in the nose and even after I had cleaned it off, I had coughed up a big gob of livery redness. This was the same – no worse, stronger.

'Hail Mary full of grace. Hail Mary full of grace.'

He was breathless between the sentences, unable to finish the prayer.

'The Lord is with you,' I said into myself.

'Hail Mary full of grace. Hail Mary full of grace. Ah fuck, it hurts. Fuck, it hurts.'

I looked around as though expecting a priest or God or the devil himself to spring from the upholstery. Prayer and profanity clashed. It was more shocking than any wound. I prayed silently he would not pray again.

'Christ, Christ, it hurts.'

We bumped over the uneven surface where some burnt barricade's bits of metal were burnished into the melted tar. His loudest screams filled the car, making me want to close my eyes and put my fingers in my ears.

Outside was Beechmount Avenue. I heard myself breathe. This was familiar ground. From here on I had explored every side street and back alley – we called them entries. There was our scout hall in Shields Street and Kennedy's bakery where, on the way to school, we would jump up to gather dough sticking to the window grills. This would be rubbed in the hands and hardened to throw later at each other in class. Almost opposite the avenue was the Broadway, the cinema where I escaped into the primary colours and sweet storyboards of Disney's films before submerging, blinking, into the grey light of the city. One of its seven rivers, the Blackstaff, the 'Blackie' to us, flowed under the road.

My uncle pressed hard on the accelerator, the engine labouring as the Falls swept up again past the Presbyterian church which the adults always seemed to be confusingly proud of, its congregation's ability to worship a sign that locals were somehow not as bigoted as Protestants.

The Beehive Bar was on one side of the road and Paddy Hynd's on the other. Broadway sloped off to the right. In the front room of a little house there, I attended piano lessons each Saturday morning with Miss Theresa McCarthy, a kindly woman who tolerated my disinterest with infinite patience. I imagined the notes on the piano, so shiny and polished. I could hear myself play exercise scales.

Now I could see the lights of the hospital ahead. They

were the only lights the length of the road. The red-brick wall of the hospital on one side and the opposite big basalt-black wall of 'the Dominican', a convent school with its enormous rose stained-glass window, formed an open canyon. With my mother, I had been caught there one night when shooting broke out. She held me close to the wall as bullets pinged and zinged overhead. A chill ran the length of my spine.

St Paul's was on the corner of my grandmother's street. There I had been baptised and had my first confession, Holy Communion and confirmation. I filled my plastic water pistols in its fonts, my grandmother lived in the shadow of its parochial house.

Directly across the road was the entrance to the hospital, the way into the casualty department stacked in sandbags in case it came under attack, soldiers stationed inside and on the roof.

The car stopped so quickly my head almost touched the man's seat in front. I pressed myself back into my own seat as my uncle got out.

'I'll get help,' was all he said, and he was away. The man breathed heavily, my own breathing patterning his, and him seemingly unaware of my presence. I do not know how long we were there, otherwise silent. Steam from the man was clouding the windows again. I tried not to move. I feared blinking.

My uncle was back.

'They won't open the doors. They won't open the doors.'

Panic for the first time edged his voice.

He was back behind the wheel. The engine spluttered over, easy because it was hot.

The man reacted, not as I expected with another scream or curse, but with something more guttural, a groan quaking through his deep being. We moved off. My uncle wiped the inside of the windscreen with the sleeve of his coat and stared ahead. We turned right onto the Grosvenor Road and then pulled across to the gate in the wall.

Just beyond there, the pigeon-stained Queen Victoria was on her throne, holding an orb, sitting, it seemed, in judgement on the poor of Belfast as they came and went with their ailments and visits to the infirm. The statue was under a canopy that let in a deathly ethereal light. I never liked looking at it because it was frightening. I imagined her coming to life, standing up, frowning at me directly.

'Christ.' It was my uncle, not the man. 'It's shut.'

The car hardly stopped before it was rolling again down the hill to the far gates. These too were locked.

'Ah Jesus. Jesus.'

Pain was overwhelming him.

My uncle made a full swinging U-turn, retracing our route back up to the main entrance.

Again he got out. Again the man and I sat, each alone.

He was praying again, this time almost into himself, mumbling rather than speaking the words. I recognised the prayer from the cadence of the hum. When he reached the phrase 'now and at the hour of our death', he stopped.

'You'll be okay.'

It was as if someone else, not me, was speaking. My voice surprised us both, I think. He started, then made a series of staccato turns, fumbling to shield his side, looking at me for the first time.

'Och son, I didn't see you. It hurts.'

'I know,' I said. What else could I say? 'You'll be okay.'

His door opened. My uncle was back.

'I got the soldiers. They're letting us in. Come on.'

My uncle had his arm and was trying to pull him to his feet. Leaning forward I could see he was bigger than I had thought. One leg was out of the car on the ground, but he was rocking against the pain in an attempt to stand.

'Christ. Christ.'

I leaned forward and put my hand to try to help him up, out, away.

My hand touched him without thinking.

'Aw Jesus. Fuck. Jesus.'

I pressed back into the seat again and in that moment he was gone, a silhouette shape, one man helping another, fading towards the chink of light 20 yards away across the pavement.

I could feel it on my hand where I had touched him, tacky and disgusting. I did not look, could have seen nothing in the dark anyway.

A car passed. I was alone. I realised my uncle had not completely closed the door.

My chest pounded. I heard the rain beads hit the windscreen and hit the road. I could not move. I feared someone was going to come to the car and blame me. I was there, there was my hand, there was this man who was going to die. My grandmother's house was at most thirty seconds away. I did not look in that direction. I could not move. Time passed.

The door opening jarred me. My uncle was back.

'They just wanted to know where we found him.'

He was turning the wheel, pulling the passenger door

closed, swinging across the road to my grandmother's street.

We got out and walked inside, the warmth making me realise I was shivering. There was a clatter of talk, my uncle explaining to my grandmother what had happened and her fussing.

She asked my uncle for his name.

He looked at her blankly, his eyes away on the memory.

'I don't know,' he told her.

She turned the radio on and within quarter of an hour we were hearing the pips count down to the bulletin.

'Good evening. This is the Radio Ulster news.' There was the briefest of pauses. 'A man has been admitted to the Royal Victoria Hospital with gunshot wounds. There are no further details.'

I was standing at the sink in the scullery, washing the blood from my hand.

A fortnight later, my uncle pointed to a paragraph tagged on to another story in the newspaper.

'Meanwhile, a man who was shot two weeks ago at Kennedy Way in west Belfast has died in hospital. He was married with two children.'

All I could think was 'I knew he would.'

The nightmares did not start until I was sixteen. I would sit bolt upright in bed, staring at the shape imprinted on my mind's eye, the man through the rain and windscreen wipers. Sweat was cold on my back. The image, always consistent, visited periodically over the following years. There was a discomfort, I put it no stronger, to being in a car on a rainy night.

If truth be told, that night directed my path. I became

a journalist, wanting always to add those 'further details' and cursing when I fell short. Sometimes my uncle and I would talk of the man, reliving the intimacy of that so exclusive journey.

The nightmares continued, gradually holding less terror than a daily working reality disproportionately spent standing at white tapes. One day I had a conversation with a policeman. I told him the story of the nameless man.

'You have no chance of finding him,' he told me. Records from the seventies had rotted.

Half an hour later he called me.

'You'll never guess what I've just found?'

Andersonstown Barracks was being demolished. Dated February 1973, a book from B Division was on top of one of the boxes of paperwork that had been moved. Entries told the story of two weekend shootings on successive nights, both at Kennedy Way. The man shot on the Saturday died a fortnight later. The man shot on the Sunday evening? He lived.

He gave me the survivor's name. Tracing him, I discovered he had never worked again after the shooting. His injuries were too severe. I did not make any attempt to speak to him, for whatever he could recount was not my story. Unquestionably, it was more terrible, much more pain-invested than any momentary trauma experienced by an accidental witness.

The nightmares stopped, overnight.

Some years later, the man died. My uncle saw the death notice in the paper. He felt compelled to go to the funeral of this man he had saved from death. He knew no one in the church. No one there knew him as he listened to the priest speak of the man's life after the shooting. He saw the holy water sprinkled on the lid, smelt the incense and watched grandchildren bear the coffin out for burial and, yes, he knew the man's name.

These Women

I write this final chapter neither as an afterthought nor a postscript. Unlike the rest of these accounts, some of it rests beyond my experience. I record it here because it is about the people who were vital to my set-up for life.

It begins with a woman I never knew. My paternal grandmother's heart gave out a fortnight after I was born. She knew me, she held me when I arrived into the world. It was the news of the Kelters baby that dominated Linden Street rather than the Cuban missile crisis which had peaked to dominate world headlines.

A more immediate, more important, crisis from a different age had prompted my grandmother's people, originally from Glenavy near the shores of Lough Neagh, to go to Belfast when it was not long a city, sometime just before the turn of the century. Sarah Ann Kernaghan was one of only two survivors from thirteen siblings, all the rest dying in infancy. At first, with her sister and parents, she lived at Abercorn Street North, then moved around the corner to Leeson Street, off the Falls.

Rural practices could never replicate the numbers demanded by the city's booming textile industry. It was the only avenue to employment for many girls, Protestant and Catholic. Firm friendships were forged in the mills.

Sarah Ann worked in a succession, among them Ewarts and Flax Street. Each morning, she joined a steady stream from the Falls. They trooped into early Mass at St Peter's, the pro-cathedral, or Clonard before clocking in at their machines where shuttles would shoot like bullets under their expert eyes. All day they would stand there, sometimes ankle-deep in the water cooling the generators, amid the deafening clacking rhythm of the spinning machines. In the spinning rooms the girls would earn just three pennies an hour.

Gradually, Sarah Ann found her way and received a promotion of sorts in the process. The mills had their hierarchy: weavers, spinners, piercers, layers, doffers, pickers. Each had a specified role and place. My grandmother became a fine damask weaver. A few sample offcuts remain as a testament to her skill.

The context is important, the atmosphere of pre-war Belfast volatile. Home Rule for Ireland was the great debate on the island and in London. Unionists were unsettled. Union leaders, James Connolly and 'Big' Jim Larkin, were at their work, organising a succession of strikes which involved both religions. Unionist factory owners did their best to foment division.

In 1913, Connolly wrote of the 'sweated women of all classes of labour in Belfast'. Three years later, one of the leaders of the Easter Rising, he was executed by the British in Dublin.

There is no way of knowing if Sarah Ann, by all accounts of a thran temperament, took part in any of the labour agitation. She was a little woman with a long stubborn streak. In later pictures taken by my father she appears frail, though there is always a thin, waspish smile. She was aged thirty-six by the time of the Dublin rebellion.

Another spate of sectarian murder was unleashed across Belfast. Republicans attacked police, army and Protestants.

Unionists, some of them police, attacked republicans and Catholics.

Sarah Ann, now married to James Kelters, moved to a house on the other side of the Falls. Under the floorboards the couple discovered grenades stored by the previous occupants. Accounts vary as to what happened to the bombs. A police cage car was ambushed in nearby Raglan Street in 1921, though guns alone inflicted the casualties. There is a distinct possibility that the grenades rotted away at the bottom of a flax dam.

The Kelters family remained unscathed through the worst of the troubles and subsequent partition and creation of the northern State. My father was born just over two years after it came into existence in law. His father, my grandfather, was 'fond of the drink'. My grandmother, four years his senior and half his size, could apparently silence him with just a look. Stocky of build, James Kelters acted as muscle for his own brother, on the docks. By virtue of his experience with machinery there and a previous stint working for the Birmingham Water Department, he was classed as a 'navvy' – a general labourer.

As the Second World War broke out in 1939 he returned from England a broken man, suffering from a severe heart complaint. He signed on for unemployment assistance from then until 12 July 1941. Refusing an offer of work in England and disallowed all benefits, for two months he brought no money into the house. His own doctor forbade him to work, certifying him able only for 'light duties'. But a Birmingham firm, desperately needing workers, secured the services of a 'medical man' who certified him fit for work.

I know these details because they were raised in Stormont, recorded in its Hansard, the parliamentary record. They were put to the Minister of Labour by a Labour MP for the Pottinger ward in east Belfast. During a dimly lit October adjournment debate, squeezed in just before business closed, Jack Beattie quoted the telegram my grandmother had received: 'Regret James Kelters died at Birmingham Infirmary on Monday.'

James Kelters had travelled to England by boat on the Thursday evening and was dead by Monday morning. My father had turned seventeen the previous day.

Pressing about my grandfather, Beattie told the House: 'The man had never started work. He was taken ill immediately after his arrival, was carted off to the infirmary and died within a short space of time. What is it all for, except because the man was drawing public assistance. The whole thing is a tragedy, and one that should not have happened. Now that it has happened, no words of mine will bring him back.' He requested compensation for the widow, my grandmother.

Saying he was 'exceedingly sorry', the minister pledged 'every assistance' possible in bringing the body home for burial.

I know little more, save that James Kelters was returned. Money remained tight. His grave in Milltown Cemetery has no stone.

My father never spoke of any of this detail. He had already been working for three years. He became the main breadwinner for the house overnight. He was always more comfortable talking about Linden Street and its people. In truth it was no different to any of the neighbouring streets, yet my father saw there a community and wider family. He would tell of the man who knocked the doors and windows every morning to waken the men and women out to the docks, factories and mills. There were police raids on three republican houses ahead of each Easter.

Part of the street's theatre, a family of three boys, to use a Belfast turn of phrase, fought the piece out when they were drunk.

'Come out and fight like men,' proclaimed one in invitation, in the middle of the street, in the middle of one night. He adopted an exaggerated Marquess of Queensbury stance, arms outstretched, knuckles upturned. When not drinking, the brothers, well-read all, could be excessively polite.

Curtains along the street twitched.

Then a door opened. The other two brothers emerged. One pinned the would-be challenger's arms from behind while the other pounded his stomach, leaving him in a winded heap on the cobbles before running back and slamming the door.

Curtains twitched closed. Neighbours went back to sleep.

The brothers' mother subsequently approached my father to put a shilling in the meter. Only after he had turned the dial did she confide she planned to 'do herself in'. Panicked, he waited until a son returned home. My father warned him of his mother's intentions. 'It'll be quite alright, Jimmy, you can go now,' the son said. An affected higher tone, almost English in accent, always delivered the words 'quite alright' when this was rehearsed. My father did return home, only to notice, two hours later, a commotion in the street.

Thinking his mother 'settled', the son had left the house. 'She turned on the gas and put her head in the oven,' my father said with a shake of his head. All attempts at resuscitation failed.

It seemed my father was deeply shocked, more by the son leaving than the manner of the mother's death. Neighbours shrugged. 'It was bound to happen someday son, so it was,' concluded one.

I know there was no money, as my grandfather was more generous with his pay packet in the bars than at home. Once, my father softly told me that for Christmas he was given an apple and orange. For an only child like me, spoiled routinely, this was an extraordinary revelation. I got the impression my father felt his own father overly strict, hard maybe, certainly quick-tempered though never violent at home, where he would sulk off the drink.

There was a pointed difference to my father's regard for his mother. He spoke of her only with deep fondness and devotion, questioning only her cooking. In turn, her biggest trauma in life came when he was almost claimed by tuberculosis.

And, with the exception of the Stormont record, all of this I know mostly because of one person. Brigid Malone was a spinster who lived a few doors opposite in Linden Street with her older sister Mary, who also had never married. Brigid was a mill girl too, having served her time also as a damask weaver in Charters just down the Falls, as well as Adams', McDonnell's in south Belfast and Elliott's off the nearby Springfield Road. With another Linden Street neighbour, Christine 'Teenie' McCullough, she and my grandmother made up an unbreakable triangle who faced the hardest of times with fortitude, friendship and faith.

Teenie – Daly was her maiden name – worked in York Street and Greves' mills. In the latter she may well have been alongside my grandmother. She married Bobby McCullough on a Christmas Day, popular for weddings because of the holiday – my grandparents married in St Peter's on Christmas Day 1917. The McCulloughs had four children: Delia, Pat, Jim, who died at six months of age, and Mary.

I never knew Teenie. She died almost a decade before I was born. My father said she and Brigid were like other mothers to him and that he was never more at home than in both their houses.

I did know Bobby McCullough, the kindest, most gentle influence on a young child. He and my father both followed Belfast Celtic and, during the football season, would be found together at home game Saturdays on the terraces of Celtic Park, a football ground in the St James' area further up the Falls Road.

Only recently did I discover Bobby had been in the Fianna, the junior IRA. He was a 'runner' – a conveyor of messages and ammunition – in a small group who made it to Dublin for the Easter Rising. Whatever he saw there, whatever happened, he turned his back on all activism and politics when he returned home to Belfast. Never did I hear him raise his voice. His funeral was the first I recall attending. I remember only not understanding why Bobby McCullough was not smiling at me from his coffin or making to pat my head, as was his custom.

A month before Bobby died, in 1966, John Scullion was

shot by a loyalist gang near Clonard Street. It is regarded by many Catholics as the first killing of the most recent Troubles. My father and mother both independently knew him from St Paul's school. 'A quiet, innocent lad,' they said. I would have been four at the time and have no recollection of the murder being mentioned.

When Sarah Ann died, Brigid Malone filled all voids. A big woman, always possessed of the jolliest of ways, she nursed me and steered my mother back to full health after a difficult pregnancy. As I grew, I saw that when Brigid would visit my maternal grandmother it was like an encounter between royal matriarchs.

They were at odds, in ways. Brigid lived 'down the road' and my grandmother 'up the road'. The Springfield junction was always an unspoken demarcation line of social significance. My grandmother could have a certain not-to-be-crossed sharpness, whereas Brigid was softer and saintly. My grandmother baked and sewed. Brigid knitted and crocheted. However, they were united in one thing: total indulgence of me.

The baking might have taken place for hours at my grandmother's ahead of Brigid's arrival which, unlike other visitors, always seemed pre-arranged. My grandmother preened, presenting buns and all types of cakes on stacked triple-decked plates, newly shone. Tea was sipped from the finest patterned cups, clinking gently on matching saucers.

After Brigid's sister died, the youngest of the McCulloughs, Mary, went to live with her, taking care of her while finding her own way working as a city-centre hairdresser. An amateur film-maker with a Super 8mm camera and a great eye, Mary would accompany Brigid to my grandmother's house to project films of our holidays onto a wall where a framed picture had been removed for exactly that purpose.

The joint holidays started as a device to enable Brigid to care further for my mother that first summer after my birth. There are photographs of me sitting in a donkey's half-filled turf basket on a Connemara day. They stayed in a bed and breakfast in Galway city.

From then on it was natural when we went away that Brigid and Mary accompanied us.

We lived for those breaks, carefree, remembered always as sunny. While my father worked at Mackie's, the holidays had to be taken in July across the Twelfth Fortnight. Year round, money was put aside to hire a car, pay for accommodation and fill a food kitty. They scoured newspaper adverts and brochures picked up from Bord Fáilte, the Republic's tourist board, and took recommendations for likely locations before agreeing on a destination.

Travelling, if we had to queue at the customs post, there would be momentary anxiety. My parents seemed to feel guilty even when they had not done any wrong. Perhaps they were thinking back to the war years when, with the advantage of the fearlessness of youth, both had been used to smuggle scarce commodities like butter, sugar and chocolate from the south. Perhaps it was something more visceral; the notion of partition, the idea of separation.

Crossing the border in the seventies, you could feel tension lift. 'That's the hard bit over,' my father would say, no matter how far we were going.

Over the years, the trips would take us back to Galway, where I watched the salmon run electric at the Claddagh

Bridge, to Kerry and all the majesty of its kingdom, and to the beaches of Tramore in Waterford and Youghal in Cork, where the people could not have been kinder.

Everywhere except Dublin, where the tourist pound was missed in its big stores, there was sympathy for the 'northerners'. In all encounters people would ask, 'What's it like in Belfast?' My father would give a resigned sigh. He could not meet the challenge.

The women on the other hand met their own challenge, patronising every craft shop along our way. My father affected chagrin.

Only once did they beat a hasty retreat. Brigid, by that stage deaf, exclaimed her thoughts through a whisper that could be heard all over the shop. 'They're charging that for one plate? Sure you'd want a whole tea set for that.'

My mother and Mary turned red as the owner stared at them. They quickly guided Brigid, still protesting the price, back to the car. My father and I were already ahead, overcome with laughter.

More giggles struck in the stately setting of Powerscourt House in County Wicklow. A busload of American tourists disembarked at the pet cemetery just as Brigid loudly remarked that one dog, according to its headstone epitaph, had 'gone hunting and never returned'. The visitors seemed to think our laughter inappropriate.

Whatever was going on in Belfast, those trips south were infused with laughter. They were the happiest of times and it was on these holidays that I gradually came to learn more about that side of my family.

Brigid told me of my grandmother's little ways, the smile, her kindness and day trips by train to Carlingford and Cooley, just south of the border near Newry. Both women, oddly, had ties of family and friendship there. Some of Brigid's relatives came from Gyles' Quay and she was able to describe the area and her annual pilgrimage to the Marian well at Faughart across the main Dundalk road. My grandmother's family had taken in a young girl from Annaverna in the Cooley mountains because of some tie to her family. She lived with them until, in her teens, she got on a ship for America. Her one visit back to Linden Street before I was born was not happy, complaining of everything being small and the lack of TV programmes, and wearing a 'housecoat' until almost midday.

One evening Brigid and I sat in a caravan in Tramore. My parents and Mary had gone to the parish hall where the priest served as the bingo caller. Aged just ten, I was happy to stay with Brigid. She sang me the songs of her youth, the songs sung by my grandmother and her while weaving. Her timing, I could see, synchronised with a mechanical memory. She told me of the Great Famine of 1847, a story handed on to her by her mother, who experienced it first-hand.

And she shared the secrets of Linden Street. There were 'hard times after the second war so there were, even after your granda died,' she said.

In the warmth of the caravan she recounted what happened in the winter of 1947. 'It was terrible,' she said. 'The snow was everywhere. It was worse nearly than the year you were born. You could hardly get out to the shops at the end of the street. Slipping and sliding everywhere, we were.'

Again, there was no money. A post-war glut meant a downturn in the big markets hit the little streets. Brigid and Sarah Ann were laid off in January, snow coming in huge drifts the following month. 'Your granny and me talked about it. There was all this fuss about the Welfare State. We'd paid our stamps, so we had, so we decided to go to the brue.'

The welfare office bureau was known to generations in Belfast as the 'brue' or 'dole'.

In her deafness Brigid spoke without interruption or questions from me to break her flow. 'The money the young ones have now? We hadn't 2d for a ticket.'

Unable to countenance squandering pennies for a bus fare, they resolved to walk together to the benefit office. The particular office they had to report to was on the opposite side of the city in east Belfast.

'I think it was somewhere up the Newtownards Road I think,' Brigid said. 'It was an awful long way, I know that. It seemed to take hours to get there. We nearly fell a lot of times.'

Shawls barely shielded them from a cutting wind.

'We weren't halfway there and we were shivering. We laughed because your granny was a lot smaller than me and I said she was using me to plough the way for her. It wasn't funny then, mind you. By the time we got there we were foundered so we were.'

In those conditions it must have taken them at least an hour and a half to reach their destination.

Brigid described the office, her eyes wandering back to the journey. 'A man on the door took pity and let us in just before shutting the door. Oh, it was a grand place inside, it was, with this big long wooden counter. There was a big long queue because only one wee window was open. We were right at the end.'

Steam rose from a line made up of women. There were other mill girls they knew, most from west Belfast.

'We sort of just nodded to each other because of the cold. There was no heat on our side of the desk but thank God it was warmer inside. It took a while to get to the window. Your granny and I went up together when we were called and there was this wee man sitting there behind a big shelf on his side of the counter so there was. He looked like a bit of a nerp, the kind that would have been a spinning master. You know the type.'

'Nerp' was the strongest word I ever heard Brigid employ, so I grasped the situation at the desk must have been serious.

'We told the wee man we were all paid up, had the stamps in our book to show him,' said Brigid. 'Your granny did the talking. She was good at that. She was a great wee woman, very strong you know, she was, in her own way.'

The man's reaction was not as they had hoped.

'His wee face went a kind of puce colour. He just shouted at us "sorry, no dole" and then slammed the window shut in our faces. We were mortified, so we were, penniless. It was dark outside and it took us even longer to get back. I don't know how under God we got through that winter.'

A tear came to her, sparked by the dredged-up humiliation. I felt guilty for seeing it, but she did not notice my embarrassment or the little diamond running down her cheek. Brigid would never admit it, but the women went hungry for days, using their money to feed others in their care.

'Oh, they straightened it out at long last,' said Brigid. 'We knew we were paid up and we went back again earlier in the day. It was a big relief to get some money, so it was. It wasn't that much but it tided us over.'

Many years later, a university politics lecturer set an essay question on the topic of 'You should be thankful to the State'. I could think only of Brigid's summer-evening story and set it to the page. The tutor handed back the essay, refusing to mark it as too personal.

I was thankful, not to the State, but to Brigid for her patience, kindness and rearing, and for coming, through her, to learn of my grandmother. Brigid died years later, deaf, blind and hardly able to hobble from seat to scullery, the only person I have ever envied for deep qualities.

After her burial I turned to look back at the grave. My father stood there, last and alone that August day, thumbing his beads, tears streaming, the only time I ever saw him cry.

These were the people who gave me foundations in life, the people I knew growing up in a timeless place that remains in my mind but which would soon change in reality. Through Brigid Malone, I felt I knew Sarah Ann. Both women, and many of those mentioned in these accounts, have stayed with me through every trial in life. Others may see them as ordinary. I do not. I rely on them still and see them flicker in the amateur camera frames recorded a lifetime ago.

They are the richest waving flares in my Belfast aurora. I am thankful for all of them.